TRANSCENDENT LOVE

The Restoration of
A Broken Marriage

CAROLYN LEE

Copyright © 2024 Carolyn Lee
Scripture quotations marked (KJV) are taken from the King James Version, public domain. Scripture quotations marked (NKJV) are taken from the New King James Version®. Copyright© 1982 by Thomas Nelson, Inc. Used by permission. All rights reserved. Scripture quotations marked (AMP / AMPC) are taken from the Amplified® Bible, Copyright© 1954, 1958, 1962, 1964, 1965, 1987 by the Lockman Foundation Used by Permission. (www.Lockman.org). Scripture quotations are taken from the Holy Bible, New Living Translation (NLT), copyright ©1996, 2004, 2015 by Tyndale House Foundation. Used by permission of Tyndale House Publishers, Carol Stream, Illinois 60188. All rights reserved. Scripture quotations marked TPT are from The Passion Translation®. Copyright © 2017, 2018, 2020 by Passion & Fire Ministries, Inc. Used by permission. All rights reserved. ThePassionTranslation.com. No part of this document may be reproduced or transmitted in any form or by any means, electronic, mechanical, photocopying, recording, or otherwise, without prior written permission of the author.

Transcendent Love
The Restoration of a Broken Marriage

Carolyn Lee
carolmosby1130@gmail.com

ISBN 978-1-949826-71-5

Printed in the USA.
All rights reserved
Published by: EAGLES GLOBAL BOOKS | Frisco, Texas
In conjunction with the 2024 Eagles Authors Course
Cover & interior designed by DestinedToPublish.com

ENDORSEMENTS

Pastor Carolyn Lee's Gift of Empathy, Wisdom, Directness and Honesty enables an individual to see situations and circumstances from different perspectives. Her key ingredient is Trust in God, which she emphasizes through her endurance; it is evident trust is her assurance.

Karen Jackson, Director of Outreach WMF Ministry

As you read Pastor Carolyn's paragon from her Heavenly Father, your life will be inspired and impacted by her love and urgent wisdom that encourages us all to submit ourselves unto God, trust and follow Jesus, and walk in the Spirit, as these steps are paramount to walking in victory. Congratulations, Carolyn! My best friend for more than 50 years, whose friendship has always been genuine, consistent, present, loving, and truthful.

Minister Sharon Perkins

Dear Pastor Carolyn,

I have no doubt this book will minister to thousands of people. You are my friend, prayer partner, sister in Christ, and my confidant. You are an amazing woman, wife, mother, and woman of God. Thank you for the important roles you've played in my life; spiritually we have come this far by faith. I see you as a blooming rose that keeps getting bigger and better. You have always been that spiritual light in my life and the light of my family. Pastor Carolyn, I am here because you were there, and you obeyed God. Thank you for always sharing your platform. I truly Love You!

Minister Dorothy Mathews

DEDICATION

Abba Father, I give you all Glory, Honor and Praise! Father I dedicate my whole being to you. I address this book to my husband, Allen Sr. I am so proud of the man you have become. Your love and dedication to God is the foundation of our family. The daily example you set by rising early to pray, study, and worship is a remarkable confirmation and living proof that God has transformed your life.

Our marriage is truly a testimony of God's Transcendent Love! To God be the Glory for more than 50 years of marriage!! With all the Love I can humanly give.

— Your Love Forever, Carolyn

ACKNOWLEDGMENTS

LaTasha Shanice was born in 1973,
which means God's Complete Perfection and Divine Order.

DeKisha Carol was born in 1975,
which means God's Complete Grace.

Allen II was born in 1978,
which means God's Complete and New Beginning.

God was aware of what our family would endure and prophesied the outcome with the birth of each of our precious children. I could not shield you from every blow life would bring, but Glory to God; He held you in the palm of His hands!

My prayer is that you fulfill God's will for your lives. As your mother, I nurtured you with the word of God. Allow that word to work inside of you. It's an honor and privilege to be your mother, and I am so proud of each of you. My love for you will continue even when my assignment on the earth is over. My love will ring throughout eternity for the three precious angels whom God entrusted me to direct in this earthly life!!

Love Forever, Mom

Tasha, you have always taken your role as the eldest seriously. You are a blessing to our family in so many ways. Thank you for your encouragement in every way you could give it! This assignment is possible because of your love and support.

My grandson Ja'Quese, since you were an infant in your baby carrier dressed in a suit and tie with a belt, the giftings and calling of God have been upon your life. I anticipate the full manifestation of everything God has promised! Embrace the call; it shall come to pass. You have been such a great support during this process. I don't have words to express my gratitude. I am forever grateful to you.

Jaime, our daughter-in-love, and our specially loved grandchildren, my prayer is that the wisdom and knowledge about God that we have imparted to you all will be handed down for generations to come. We love you dearly!

Special recognition to my sisters, Ora, Debra, Sharon, and Linda, who intercede and encourage me as I endeavor to fulfill the will of God. I am so grateful for our weekly Sister's Ministry time.

Mama desired that our entire family know God. We have answered the call of watchmen for the Mosby family. To God be all the Glory! Forever in my heart John, Frances, Clarence, Darlean and Eva

Love your sister, Carolyn

FROM THE AUTHOR'S HEART

Compare your marriage to a beautiful wedding cake. There are unique types of wedding cakes that come in a variety of flavors. Some are quite eloquent with eye-catching decorations. Depending on the details and size, the prices can range from modest to extremely expensive.

Have you ever attended a wedding reception? Usually, the cake captures your attention. After the meal, the waiter serves slices of the wedding cake for dessert. Some are just as delicious as they look. But have you ever tasted cake where there was simply no taste? Have you ever heard it said, "That cake was beautiful, but it didn't taste good at all"?

I pray that as you read this book you will discover the ingredients that will make your marriage appetizing and gratifying. Don't forget that special ingredient of Love. My prayer is that you will be able to serve pieces of cake that will minister to other marriages. I pray couples will taste and see the miracle-working power of God displayed in your marriage.

After you have experienced the heat and endured the test of time, when you have allowed God's Transcendent Love to reach beyond your human love, then you will experience a flavor that goes beyond the natural taste. My prayer is that your marriage will be baked to perfection.

Marriage is the product of two people coming together as one, combining your backgrounds, your experiences, what you admire, your oppositions, and your perspectives. It's very important to add all the ingredients and mix them well in a large bowl of Life on medium speed. Prepare the pans with the Holy Spirit to ensure the cake will not stick and crumble when done.

The next step is very important; you must allow God to adjust the thermostat. He knows the correct temperature for your specific marriage. No matter how blazing hot the oven becomes, keep the door closed and remain inside to ensure your marriage is baked thoroughly. Also, the atmosphere that your marriage is baked in is of the utmost importance. It must be one of tranquility; this is necessary to allow all the ingredients to bake together without being disturbed. This atmosphere will prevent your marriage from sinking in the middle.

When baked to perfection according to God's timing, allow your marriage to cool. Then, yield to the Holy Spirit as the icing is applied with the spatula of prayer. Be generous with the finishing touches of sprinkles of Love and Affection.

Now your marriage is prepared to bring Glory and Honor to God! As you serve slices of your wedding cake filled with testimonies of God's Transcendent Love. As couples partake of the wonderful miracles, they will be encouraged to know what God has done in your marriage. He's willing to perform the same in theirs.

I pray that your marriage is the epitome of the covenant that God has designed it to be.

From my heart to yours,
Carolyn

CONTENTS

FOREWORD xi

INTRODUCTION xiii

CHAPTER 1: INNOCENT LOVE 1

CHAPTER 2: STARTING FROM SCRATCH 9

CHAPTER 3: NEW DISCOVERIES 14

CHAPTER 4: DRIFTING 29

CHAPTER 5: COMMUNICATION CONNECTION 41

CHAPTER 6: THE DARKEST STORM 52

CHAPTER 7: ANGELS OF ENCOURAGEMENT 76

CHAPTER 8: WHEN THE END IS THE BEGINNING 86

CHAPTER 9: STARTING OVER 97

CHAPTER 10: LOVE CONQUERS ALL 104

CHAPTER 11: AN INVITATION TO EXPERIENCE THE MIRACLE 110

FOREWORD

I am sure with the turn of every page in this book you will find and know what it is to go beyond ordinary limits of love in restoring a broken marriage. This book will emphasize the true story of Christ's love towards us and how restoration is an essential part of love in a redemptive manner concerning marriage. I have known the author for over twenty years and have witnessed the story that she lays out in this book concerning her own marriage. I am one who believes that God will make a message out of what is presumed to be our mess. I say presumed, because only God can take that which was meant to harm us and turn it around for His glory.

This book will encourage those who may be going through a broken marriage and those who are interested in knowing how broken marriages can be restored to help themselves and others reclaim what God has joined together. Carolyn Lee is a mother, grandmother, sister, Minister, Evangelist, Teacher, and Pastor who has been married for over fifty years. Her story uniquely qualifies her to write this book as a reassurance and inspiration for all of us to know that there is hope in the institution of marriage.

Transcendent Love: The Restoration of a Broken Marriage is a book of our time and beyond! It provides us with the helpful tools of not coming to quick decisions but rather listening to God and allowing Him to order our steps as we believe in His Word. Transcendent love has no bounds and no limits because it is of God. The Word tells us that *"love suffers long and is kind; love does not envy; love does not parade itself, is not puffed up; does not behave rudely, does not seek its own, is not provoked, thinks no evil; does not rejoice in iniquity, but rejoices in the truth; bears all things, believes all things, hopes all things, endures all things"* (1 Corinthians 13:4-6), and this book is the perfect example of this truth.

I was honored to officiate the vow renewal ceremony celebrating fifty years of marriage for the author and her husband. I can safely say that the Word of Christ through Mark rings true for their transcendent love, and that is, *"Therefore what God has joined together, let not man separate"* (Mark 10:9).

Ronnie Woodfork, Senior Pastor
New Life Outreach World Changing Ministries (NLOWCM)
Master of Arts MA in Ministry Studies, Moody
Theological Seminary

INTRODUCTION

We have our own ideas and intentions when it comes to marriage. It's only after we have entered this covenant-relationship that we find the goals anticipated are sometimes difficult to obtain. The purpose of this book is to enhance your perspective regarding God's purpose for your marriage. Also, this book will help you gain an understanding that God's love is efficient enough to reach beyond human barriers and perform what is impossible for you alone to execute in your marriage.

This book exposes the strategies in the spirit realm that lie in wait to destroy your marriage. It also reveals the power that God has given you to arise above every impediment that presents itself against your marriage. The word "transcendence" comes from the Latin prefix *trans*, meaning "beyond," and the word *scandare*, meaning "to climb." When you have reached the state of transcendence, you have gone beyond ordinary limitations. If you have tried everything you could think of to make things better in your marriage to no avail, while reading this book my prayer is that you will become aware of new tools that will be helpful and effective in resolving issues in your marriage.

When we fall in love with that special person, we have no idea of what we will encounter. We do not know about the twists and turns that will occur down the road as we attempt to build a life together. When the honeymoon is over and you realize it's not a dream, you will discover human love alone will not sustain your marriage. "Eros love" is the physical, sensual intimacy between a husband and wife. It expresses sexual and romantic attraction.

One day you will realize that you need God's "agape love," which is the highest form of love. Agape love is a selfless, sacrificial, and unconditional love. Agape love isn't born out of emotions, feelings, familiarity, or attraction, but from the will and as a choice to give sacrificially, even if not returned, earned, or deserved. It's impossible to experience or give this love outside of a relationship with God.

When we are trying to express how we feel or get a point across to our spouse, our words enter their ears. But when God speaks to a person, it penetrates their heart. God knows how to get our attention because God speaks with a love that transcends all barriers. God knows you and your spouse better than anyone; He is the manufacturer. Therefore, if a problem occurs with the product, we should consult the One who made it and not attempt to fix it ourselves.

As you peruse this personal testimony of the miracle that God performed in our marriage, there will be moments of reflection where you can pause and consider areas in your own marriage that could use some attention. I pray God's Transcendent Love will consume your marriage in every area according to God's Holy Covenant.

LOVE

CHAPTER 1

INNOCENT LOVE

A FAIRY-TALE BEGINNING

One hot summer night, the moon was shining oh, so bright. The wind was blowing a wonderful soft breeze, so light you could feel this would be a very special summer night.

A young man and young woman were taking a stroll in the early night. When their paths crossed, it happened as quick as a flash of speeding light. Their eyes met, and at first, they could not say a word; two hearts beating as one was the only thing that could be heard. Now, the young woman was wearing pink and white. To the young man she seemed to glow and glisten under the magnificent moonlight. The young man was tall, handsome, and dressed so neat it made the young woman feel light on her feet.

They exchanged names there under a starlit sky. You see, Cupid was present, and without any warning, the love arrows began to fly. Allen and Carolyn began to share; suddenly, they began to stare. Each one could see a twinkle in the other's eye. Something special had taken place between this teenage girl and guy.

Then the courtship began, with movies and dinner every weekend. The walks under the moonlight holding hands, singing love songs to each other as they discussed wedding plans. Allen and Carolyn were married on August 20, 1973; now all they had dreamed and talked about had finally become reality.

THE COURTSHIP

Do you remember when you met the love of your life? When you reminisce back to that day, afternoon, evening, or night, can't you remember the specific details, like how the room looked or how the weather was? Do you remember the light in their eyes and the expression on their face when you made eye contact for the first time? Don't you remember how it felt, like everything stood still and you two were all that mattered even though the room may have been filled with other people?

Well, the picture is crystal clear in my mind. Reminiscing back to the year 1970, I was 15 years old, entering my second year of high school. My family had just moved to a new apartment, and this was my first weekend home. You see, during the summer I would babysit for my cousin Emma, who lived on the South Side of Chicago.

One evening I was with my sisters Darlean and Sharon. We were walking home from a restaurant. As we approached the corner, a group of guys were walking toward us. Allen was one of those guys. You see, my sisters would go to the park and watch the young men play basketball. They were acquainted with some of the guys, and as they began to greet each other, Allen and I made eye contact. This was interrupted by my sister Darlean saying, "Carolyn, this is Allen, and Allen, this is my sister Carolyn." I recall Allen saying, "You're looking good, Carolyn." I responded, "You don't look so bad yourself, Allen." He then asked if he could come by in an hour or so, if I didn't mind, as he would like to talk to me. I said, "I guess that will be alright." He kept his word, and we sat and got acquainted with each other that warm summer night under the moonlight and stars. I must admit I enjoyed the conversation. Allen asked if he could come by the next day. The days turned into weeks, and the weeks turned into months. Most weekends we would go downtown to the movies and to dinner at Ronny's Steak House. We would go window shopping, looking at the clothes and shoes, making jokes about buying each other outfits and shoes we knew the other person wouldn't dare wear. We laughed a lot and looked forward to spending time with each other.

I remember him taking me to restaurants where live music was being played while we ate. It was romantic, and I was impressed. Another romantic thing we did while spending time together was sing love songs to each other. The songs had meaning, like "Heaven must have sent you from above, Heaven must have sent your precious love." There was no doubt about it; we were in love.

Looking back, I was too young to get so caught up in a young man. My focus should have been on school and setting goals for my future. I had no idea and no expectations of what I wanted in life. Love is a powerful force, and if you are not careful it will sweep you off your feet.

GROWING UP FAST

As a result of our love, a beautiful baby girl was born Wednesday, May 23, 1973, at 1:28 a.m. We named her LaTasha Shanice. I was in my junior year of high school when Tasha was born, but there was never any doubt in my mind about finishing school. I was determined that I had to graduate, and I had to graduate with my class. Although there was no money for senior pictures nor prom because I now had a baby, nevertheless, she would be taken care of, and she came first.

Allen began to save so we could get married. You see, there was no way my mother would agree that we could live together unless we were married. We found an apartment in a building my sisters Darlean and Debra lived in, not far from my mother.

Allen and I were married on Monday, August 20, 1973, with both of our mothers present. Allen was 19 years old, and I was 17. My mother signed, giving her consent. We were babies with a newborn baby, about to enter a full-grown world with no idea of what to expect. The only thing we knew for sure was we were in love, and at that time nothing else mattered.

GET DIRECTIONS BEFORE DRIVING INTO THE UNKNOWN

Marriage is for mature people! Marriage is not a game; it is real life with consequences. I wish we had received counsel and directions, like getting directions before you leave when driving to a location you have never been to before. Marriage is a very long road that has a lot of twists and turns.

There are mountains and valleys, bumps, and dips. You will encounter all types of weather; you will go through rain and hailstorms. The season may be summer, but that won't stop it from snowing. Don't be surprised if it's winter but flowers bloom. Marriage is unpredictable, just like the weather and seasons.

It's a great idea to sit down together and consider the cost of this lifetime commitment you are making. When life happens, and it will, you need to hold on tight to the commitment you made to each other. I can't stress enough how important it is to be totally honest with each other. Whatever secret you chose not to reveal will come to light; it could be years later, but it will be revealed. When two people truly love each other, the key to securing that love is transparency. If you can't be honest with each other in the beginning, you are already headed for trouble.

To be honest, no one offered us advice. I'm not sure if we would have listened anyway. We felt that we had it all figured out. We didn't think about a savings account or a rainy-day fund. We had no idea of a budget; all I knew was I had to finish school, and Allen knew he had to keep a job to pay the bills.

You may feel like "We got this. No one can tell us what to do with our lives." Let me assure you, if you don't get directions, you will end up in a ditch! One day you will realize and wish you had gotten a map from somebody and paid attention to the directions. To need advice and not seek or accept it is pride.

Perhaps as you read this book, you realize your marriage is in a ditch, and the directions you refused to accept or pay attention to were needed after all. I have personally experienced this while driving, thinking I was going in the right direction only to realize that I missed a turn and had to go back and find the correct exit to get back on track. That's what this book is all about. I'm praying the wrong turns we made will point you in the right direction.

You see, being in love is not enough. You can have knowledge, but if you don't have wisdom to know how to apply the knowledge, it will do you no good.

I would love to share just a little of what has been revealed to me with you. My prayer is that you will receive it in the same spirit it is given.

~PONDERING MOMENTS~

CHAPTER 2

STARTING FROM SCRATCH

THE DREAM

Every woman has dreams of a beautiful wedding with vibrant colors, beautiful flowers. Some women dream about their wedding day long before their prince charming comes along. They already have in mind who their maid of honor and bridesmaids would be.

They can see themselves in the perfect wedding gown. Strolling down the aisle as that romantic song fills the air. Picturing the man of their dreams patiently waiting for them at the altar.

When I was a little girl, one Christmas my grandfather bought me a doll, and she wore a beautiful white wedding dress. She had earrings in her ears and flowers in her hands, and she wore high-heeled shoes. That was my first picture of a wedding.

As I got older, when I thought of marriage, I would always say to myself, "When I get married, that man will be the father of all my children. I will not sleep around with Tom, Dick, and Harry, and men will not discuss me with each other."

My dream was to get married, and that is just what I did. We had already had our honeymoon and our beautiful baby girl. The only thing left to do was to get married, move into our own apartment, and play house. I had no idea of how to be a wife, and Allen didn't have a clue of what a husband was. The only thing we knew for sure was we were in love.

Monday, August 20, 1973, is a day forever etched in my memory. We hired my brother-in-law Clarence to drive Allen, myself, and our mothers to City Hall, where we were married. We were so excited about exchanging our wedding vows. We had no rings, no flowers, and no idea of what we were about to encounter. The one thing we were sure of was our love for each other. I recall my mother saying to me with concern in her voice, "Just because you have a baby by Allen doesn't mean you have to marry him." I vividly remember replying, "I don't want to marry Allen because I have a baby. I love him." With that answer, she gave me her consent and blessings.

OUR COMICAL APARTMENT

I will never forget the love shown to us as we began our new lives together. My uncle, Reverend Ben Smith Sr., was the pastor of my family church, Israel Samuel AME Zion. After finding out I was married, he called and said he wanted to do something to help. Since I was a member of the church, he had an announcement made for the members to bring gifts after service one Sunday. We had a small reception thanks to the love of my uncle.

My mother was getting new furniture, so she gave us a couch she no longer needed. The legs were broken, so we put bricks under it. She also gave us a cocktail table; the legs were loose, and if you bumped it when walking past, the whole table would lean in the direction it was bumped.

My grandmother gave us a yellow hand-painted kitchen table and four chairs. You had to be careful to pick the chairs up by the metal frames on each side. If you picked one up by the back, you would be holding the back in your hands, and the seat and metal frame would all go in different directions.

My Aunt Sophie gave us valuable instructions along with a twin-size metal bedframe. She explained it was a twin-size frame but to buy a three-quarter-length mattress to make it bigger. Following her instructions, we did just that. The bed was bigger, but the mattress hung off both sides. We had to be careful not to fall out.

Allen's mother gave us a black and white TV. It was so small, it's a good thing we were in love because we had to sit close if we wanted to watch it together. She also gave us our first Christmas tree; it was silver with a light that sat on the floor, and as it rotated and reflected on the tree it would turn yellow, green, red, and blue. It was so beautiful to us!

My Uncle James, who was my favorite uncle, purchased a brand-new refrigerator. It was the only new item we owned. I remember him saying to us, "I don't want the baby's milk in a used refrigerator. It could stop working in the night and the milk could spoil."

Yes, we laughed a lot in our first three-room apartment. Every room was filled with jokes and a whole lot of love. We didn't have much, but we had each other.

~PONDERING MOMENTS~

CHAPTER 3

NEW DISCOVERIES

DISCOVERING HOW TO EMBRACE CONSEQUENCES

My husband and I discovered that it would have been better if we had prepared by saving before we got married. Allen didn't graduate high school because he had to cross gang territory to attend school. One day, he said, while coming home the gang was chasing him and another young man. Shots began to ring out, when the young man running next to him had a bullet go through his coat. That was the last day Allen attended school. Now he had a newborn baby and a wife still in high school. One thing I can say, my husband always kept a job, even if it was day labor. I remember Pampers being .99 cents a box. We also had cloth diapers. I also recall Similac formula was approximately .79 cents a can.

I soon discovered that being married and a mother was a lot more than playing house. I made a choice, and sacrifices came with it. My senior year of high school turned out very different from what I had imagined in my freshman year. I must admit at times I wish I knew what going to prom felt like. There was no money for prom or senior pictures because there were bills to pay. I was still a teenager, but I had stepped into a grown-up world. I was determined to accomplish the task of graduating with my class. My mother was concerned that I would not finish school. I felt I had to prove to her that I could do it. I graduated in June 1974 with my husband and my mother in attendance.

One of my classes in high school was Office Occupation. In my senior year, I went to school part of the day and worked the other part. After finishing school, I was hired full-time.

There were two ladies at work; one was a Muslim and the other a Jehovah's Witness. One lady was trying hard to convince me to go to the temple. The other lady shared scriptures from the Bible that sounded familiar, but I wasn't sure of the meanings. She kept inviting me to go to the hall. To be honest, listening to them was very confusing. I said I was a Christian, but I couldn't explain what a Christian was or believed. When the Muslim lady began explaining that my body was made from the same substance the moon and stars were made of, I realized I needed to find out the truth because that didn't sound right at all.

CAROLYN LEE

DISCOVERING WHAT I KNEW ABOUT GOD

My mother told me that before I was born my grandmother asked her if she could raise one of her grandchildren. I was the sixth child born to my parents. I was six months old when my mother agreed I could live with my father's parents, Lacy and Sue Bell Collins, in Gary, Indiana. They were the first parents I knew. I called them Mama and Daddy. My grandfather was a minister; he taught me how to pray and would read the Bible to me at night. I will never forget him telling me, "The words in red are Jesus talking," and then he would continue reading. I was extremely close to my grandparents; my grandfather was my everything. When I was eight years old, I went to live in Chicago with my mother and siblings. My mom would take me to church where my grandfather Reverend Archie Henry Smith pastored, Israel Samuel A.M.E. Zion church. I still remember the choir marching in with their robes on, singing "Walk in the light, beautiful light." Many of the choir members were my cousins.

It was a tradition that all the children at the age of 12 attend a weeklong service and sit on the chairs in the front row. It was called the mourners bench. The choir would sing, and my grandfather would preach. This was a serious time; during this week I was not allowed to play outside at a certain time during the day, and my mother would have me go into a room alone to pray. Now, I had no problem praying; my grandfather had made sure of that. But after I had said the Lord's prayer three or four times, there was nothing else to say. I would just sit there in the dark until my mother said it was time to come out. Finally, Friday arrived, the last night of the revival. On this night, a chair was placed in front of each person. When my grandfather told us to sit in the chair in front of us, we switched seats. My understanding was this was an indication that you crossed over. I had no idea why I crossed over or what any of it meant.

My grandfather asked each person how they wanted to be baptized. My mother had already instructed me to say I want to be immersed like Jesus. But the majority wanted to be sprinkled, so everybody got sprinkled. My mother was not pleased; she stated it only wet my hair after she had pressed it out.

I loved to go to church. My Uncle James would pick me up on Sundays. Sometimes my mother and sisters would go, but I went every Sunday. There was a store across the street from the church. My cousin Florene Anderson would give me change to buy snacks after Sunday School every week. No doubt about it, she was my favorite cousin.

I remember the Sunday School lessons with the little cards that had pictures on the front and the lesson on the back. I remember being on the usher board; my Aunt Sophie was president. My cousin Yvonne and I were junior ushers. We spent a lot of weekends either at Yvonne's house or my house. Yvonne's older brother, who we called Bo-Bo, would give us money for snacks, and we would stay up eating, laughing, and talking into the wee hours of the morning. At 7:30 a.m. sharp, my aunt would say it was time to get up. We would be so tired, but she would remind us, "You laughed and talked all night. I didn't bother you, but now it's time for church."

I recall the words of my grandfather's favorite song, "If you make it in glory before I do, save a seat for me." When the choir would finish singing, he would say, "It makes the hair rise up on my head." Yvonne and I would laugh so hard because he had no hair.

I had attended church all my life, but now, as an adult, I was discovering I didn't understand what I thought I believed in. I had a longing to know if God was real and which God was real. The God at my church, the God at the hall of the Jehovah's Witnesses, or the God at the temple the Muslims attend.

I remember in my first year of high school there was a young lady who we called sanctified; her name was Shirley. She wore long dresses, no makeup, no jewelry, and no pants. She kept inviting me to go to church with her, and I went to an evening service. I had been experiencing stomach pains for a few weeks that were getting worse. I mentioned it to Shirley, and her mother came over to me during the service, put her hand on my stomach, and prayed. Then something strange happened: Where the pain was, a burning sensation started, and then the pain was gone. That night was my first experience with God. When the pastor asked if there was anybody there that was not saved, I raised my hand. I knew I wasn't saved because I didn't even know what it meant. I went to the altar and repented of my sins and accepted Jesus as my Savior. When I got home, I excitedly told my mother and sisters that I was saved. My sisters laughed at me and said, "You can't dance anymore, and you can't wear pants anymore. Ha, ha, Carolyn is saved!" I was already different and wanted to fit in, so I said, "Well, forget it; I'm not saved." I'll never forget that encounter with God; it is forever etched in my heart.

One Sunday, my mother felt led to attend a church within walking distance of where she lived. When the pastor prayed for healing, she felt popping in her joints and was healed of arthritis. She continued to attend because she was receiving and understanding the word of God in a way she never had before.

I began attending church with my mom. I believe that because I desperately wanted to know God, He began to reveal Himself to me. The word of God says we are drawn to God by the Holy Spirit, and I felt a strong desire to know who God was. Although I had heard the songs before, they seemed to have new meanings. The word of God was explained in a way I could understand. After sitting in Sunday services for a few weeks and attending Bible studies, I realized that I needed to accept Jesus in my heart. I never understood what a personal relationship with God meant. I believe my grandparents and my uncle taught me the best they knew, but I had never been introduced to Jesus. It was like a light shining so bright, and I had to find out more about that light.

In December 1974, I will never forget walking to the prayer room with missionary Idellar Sams. She made it very clear that if I was sincere when I repented of my sins and asked Jesus to be my Savior, my life would never be the same. I prayed that Sunday morning in the prayer room at New Evangelical Bible Church. I didn't see any stars, but something happened that I don't have words to explain, and my life changed forever.

I Discovered That God Was REAL.

I was so excited to attend the Wednesday night mid-week service. The Sunday before, I had invited Jesus into my heart as my Lord and Savior. Now my prayer was, "God, show me that You are real." I had been so confused that I wanted to make sure I was on the right track. With everything in me, I wanted to know God.

"Then (with a deep longing) you will seek Me and require Me (as a vital necessity) and (you will) find Me when you search for Me with all your heart" (Jeremiah 29:13, AMP).

At the end of service, Pastor Sams said if anyone wanted prayer they could come to the altar. I remember saying over and over in my mind as I walked down the aisle, "God, please show me that You are real." I recall Pastor Sams putting his hand on my shoulder; I don't remember what he prayed. When he was done, he said, "Lift your hands and say thank you, Jesus." I lifted my hands and began to say, "Thank you, Jesus," as instructed. I felt a joy that I never knew existed! Mere words could not explain what I was experiencing. It felt like something was turning over and over deep down in my chest.

The more I said, "Thank you, Jesus," the faster it turned, and the more joy I could feel. I had an encounter with God that night; God continued to reveal Himself to me. I was convinced beyond any doubt that Jesus was my Savior and GOD WAS REAL!

"Blessed are those who hunger and thirst for righteousness, for they shall be filled" (Matthew 5:6, NKJV).

BEWARE OF IMITATIONS
~ A MOMENT OF REFLECTION ~

John 15:1 says, *"Jesus is the true vine."*

If Jesus is the true vine, we must beware of the false vine.

Everything that appears real is not always authentic. Wherever there is something real, you will always find a counterfeit. For example, when shopping for jewelry, you don't want something that's not real because when you wear it a few times it will begin to turn its true color. If that is true in the natural, it's also true in the spiritual.

When God said in Genesis 1:26, NKJV *"Let us make man in our image, according to Our likeness,"* God blew into man the breath of life, which was part of Himself, and man became a living soul. When man sinned in the garden, the spirit that God blew inside of man died. Ever since that time, there has been a void inside of man which he seeks to fill. There is a constant search, a hunger that can't be satisfied. There is a deep hole; no matter where man turns, no matter how much alcohol, drugs, sex, or money he has, he will never be filled. That longing and desire is the part of God that He put on the inside of man that needs to be revived or born again. There is only one way for that to happen. Man must first recognize that he is separated from God, repent of his sins, and accept Jesus as his Savior and Lord.

"There was a man named Nicodemus, a Jewish religious leader who was a Pharisee. After dark one evening, he came to speak with Jesus.

'Rabbi,' he said, 'we all know that God has sent you to teach us. Your miraculous signs are evidence that God is with you.' Jesus replied, 'I tell you the truth, unless you are born again, you cannot see the Kingdom of God.' 'What do you mean?' exclaimed Nicodemus. 'How can an old man go back into his mother's womb and be born again?' Jesus replied, 'I assure you, no one can enter the Kingdom of God without being born of water and the Spirit. Humans can reproduce only human life, but the Holy Spirit gives birth to spiritual life'" (John 3:1-6, NLT).

THERE IS NO WAY AROUND IT; WE MUST BE BORN AGAIN!

The only way man can come to this realization is by hearing the word of God. Because faith comes by hearing the word of God. The Bible says we will know the truth, and the truth will set us free. If we hear and receive a lie that pertains to God, we will be deceived, and the void deep inside will not be filled with the true God but a false God. You may ask, how can I tell who the true God is? I'm glad you asked. Everything concerning the true and living God will line up with His written word. The rule of thumb is that whatever is presented to you, and it does not matter who presents it, if it's not written in the word of God (The Holy Bible), do not receive it! You may also hear some say Jesus was just a good man, but the Bible says Jesus is the Son of God, and the only way to God is through His Son. If you attempt to initiate a relationship with God, any other way you are like a thief or robber.

To attend church is not enough; you need to know what that church's doctrine is. It must be based on the virgin birth and the death and resurrection of Jesus Christ. It can have a cross on top and a Bible verse below it, but if the church does not teach the complete word of God, run! Many times, the word of God is taken out of context and twisted to say what someone wants it to say. That's why we should not take anyone's word at face value, but we should study ourselves. The Bible says we should study to show ourselves approved, rightly dividing the word of God. It has been said the Bible is full of contradictions, but let me assure you that if you study the word of God, do not just read the Bible but instead get a good study Bible. Learn how to navigate words in Greek and Hebrew, and become competent in using the concordance. I promise you will find there are no contradictions. The problem is that people attempt to study the Bible like they would a textbook.

The Bible is not a textbook nor a novel; it is the God-breathed living word of God penned by men through the inspiration of God Himself. Therefore, if a spiritually dead person attempts to study the living word of God, they will never understand it because they are spiritually dead! The Bible says we must worship God in spirit and in truth; it is a spirit-to-spirit connection.

When you are searching for God, beware of getting in every prayer line and receiving every prophecy. Just as you are particular about eating from different restaurants, be careful of the church you receive from. Many people are seeking a word from God, but they are looking to receive that word from a man. Don't get me wrong, God does speak through men, but if the word given does not line up with the written word of God, it is a false word. Seek God for yourself. I promise He will give you the word you are seeking.

2 Timothy 3:16 (AMPC) says, *"Every Scripture is God-breathed (given by His inspiration) and profitable for instruction, for reproof and conviction of sin, for correction of error and discipline in obedience, (and) for training in righteousness (in holy living, in conformity to God's will in thought, purpose, and action."*

The scripture says that all scripture is God-breathed, meaning the word of God is the breathing out of God Himself. John 6:63b (NKJV) says, *"the words that I speak to you are spirit, and they are life."* Breath and spirit mean the same thing; therefore, it's not the black or red letters in the Bible that give life, but the spirit who is the essence of those words. Once this is understood, we come to the Bible not to gain head knowledge but to be touched by the spirit, which is the life-giving essence of the word. If we open our spirits to the word of God, the spirit of God will then impart new life and understanding of Himself to our spirits. This can never be obtained in the natural world; it can only become reality if we receive it by faith and become born again.

A person can attend a church where the genuine word of God is being taught. They can accept Jesus, but if they never make Him Lord of their lives, they will live defeated. They must be taught that when they invite Jesus to be Lord of their lives, it means to acknowledge His ownership, and they must give up their rights. They must be discipled and taught how to walk in the spirit. To say, "Jesus, come into my heart and forgive me of all my sins," is the very beginning. Just saying words are not enough. God wants our whole heart. Revelation 3:15 says God would rather we be hot or cold because if we are lukewarm, it makes Him nauseated. Everyone must develop a personal relationship with God. The only way to do that is to spend time in His word through prayer and worship. You must be willing to develop a relationship with God. How badly do you really want to know God? Are you willing to surrender every part of your life? We must surrender ALL because God will not accept anything less.

Pastors, ministers, and teachers will be held accountable for leading souls to God and then leaving them on their own to sink or swim. People must be taught; they should be taken by the hand and shown how to walk according to the word of God! Does it take time? Yes, it does. Will you have to sacrifice? Yes, you will. Pastors, ministers, and teachers have a very important responsibility according to God's plan. They are servants. Jesus is our example, and He was a servant.

"My brethren, let not many of you become teachers, knowing that we shall receive a stricter judgment," (James 3:1, NKJV).

Speaking of imitation, people themselves must be real before they can receive the real. As my pastor, Ronnie Woodfork, often says, "It's time to stop playing church and be the church. People want to live dirty then die clean." People want to live their lives the way they want to, then when things go wrong, they expect God to rescue them. It doesn't work like that. If you are not praying and reading God's word and do not have an intimate relationship with Him when everything is well, why do you want to contact Him when things are going wrong? God is not Let's Make a Deal or Burger King. People tend to make God promises: "If You do that for me, I'll do this for You." Then, when things get better, they forget all about the promises they made.

"It is better that you should not vow than that you should vow and not pay" (Ecclesiastes 5:5, AMPC).

CAROLYN LEE

~PONDERING MOMENTS~

CHAPTER 4

DRIFTING

DRAWING CLOSER TO GOD

Drifting is a slow steady movement from one place to another or a gradual change or development from one situation to another, especially to something bad.

We were excited to welcome our second daughter, DeKisha Carol, on Thursday, September 18, 1975, at 10:03 a.m. You see, this was another occasion where God demonstrated His mighty power to me. The doctors induced my labor at approximately 9:30 a.m. due to my water breaking the night before. The doctor indicated it would probably be late evening before I delivered. Lying there, I recalled the missionaries praying for me at church, saying, "It won't be much longer before you deliver your baby. God told me to tell you that when you go into labor, ask him for whatever you want, and he will perform it." I looked at the clock then looked up at the ceiling and reminded God of what

He spoke through the missionaries. I prayed and asked God to let my baby be born within an hour. When I tried to tell them the baby was coming, the nurses said it was too soon. When they finally checked, everybody started rushing and saying the baby is coming! God is an on-time God, and He will do everything He promised!

My father, Clarence Mosby Sr., transitioned on October 23, 1975, and my mother, Miley Mosby, transitioned on January 4, 1976. This was a very difficult time in my life. I had a lot of unanswered questions. I was 19 years old, married, with two children and no parents. I was grateful to still have my grandmother, Sue Bell Collins. Tasha and Kisha spent time with her in the summer. God was faithful to surround me with women of God to advise me as a mother while raising my children.

My mom loved ALL her grandchildren so much. She received a diagnosis of colon cancer and still insisted on her grandchildren not going to babysitters but staying with her until she absolutely could no longer care for them.

I remember teaching the Primary Sunday School class with Tasha sitting in a chair next to me and Kisha in her carrier seat at my other side. We were at the hospital a lot with Tasha. She was our first baby, but with Kisha, I was learning to pray, anoint with oil, and speak the word of God over her. Yes, I was developing a closer relationship with God, for sure.

DRIFTING AWAY

I desired to attend church as a family, but my husband was not interested. He didn't understand what had happened to the young woman he married. I was told by my pastor that I needed to change the way I dress. I didn't wear pants, and my earrings had to be small. I wore no makeup at all; my desires were no longer the same, and neither were my looks. I would no longer sip a little wine to fit in, and I never experienced being drunk. I was never a smoker, even though my best friend Sharon and I would buy a pack of cigarettes and smoke while coming home from school.

When we reminisce as adults, we laugh because at the time neither one of us knew that we couldn't wait to get home because we were both dizzy and nauseated, but we put up a good front while we were together. We would dress in the same colors. I'll never forget the red, white, and blue jeans with bold stripes. With the choker pullover tops that had little buttons on the side. One of us would wear red and the other white; we were cool.

When a relationship begins to drift apart, it's so subtle you don't even realize it. It's an unconscious process of gradually moving away. Deep inside the love is there, but the time you spend together is not the same. You go through the motions, but you can sense something is missing.

In the beginning, Allen and I were inseparable. We did everything together. Now that I was developing a relationship with God, I didn't even consider my husband. I'll never forget the Sunday I came home and told him I was saved. Confused, he replied, "But you always go to church."

As time goes on in a marriage, if you are not careful you can take each other for granted. Going to the movies and walking under the moonlight was no longer happening. A woman desires attention and affection, especially after two pregnancies. Your body changes, and the size you once wore is a vague memory. Your emotions are all over the place, and you don't have a clue what's happening. I recall my mother saying, "A woman experiences so many changes in her body, sometimes she does not have the words to express how she feels."

A man desires emotional support, encouragement, and most of all respect. When a man is disrespected by his wife, if it's not recognized and corrected, the marriage is headed for trouble. When the woman is upset, the entire household is upset. When the woman is at peace, the entire household is at peace. Women must learn to be quiet; always having the last word is not wise. Women are the atmosphere setters; the thermostat is in their possession. Women must study to be quiet, according to 1 Thessalonians 4:11. You may have worked hard to build your marriage, but negative words will destroy it. The husband may be the strongest physically, but the woman holds the power when it comes to influence, which must be used carefully. God gave woman this power, but beware; it can be used both positively and negatively. When situations arise, God will give you strategies to navigate and conquer each one. The only way you will fail is if your method is of yourself and not God's way of doing things.

"A wise woman builds her home, but a foolish woman tears it down with her own hands" (Proverbs 14:1, NLT).

A woman can build a man up or tear him down, but remember, if you tear him down, you allow room for another woman to build him up. I guarantee neither my husband nor I knew how to do any of these things. You see, we had no idea of what we needed ourselves, so how could we supply what the other person needed? Everything we experienced, we had to learn from the school of hard knocks. We had to figure it out at each turn, holding on to each other as we navigated through life.

YOU NEED AN ANCHOR

Anchors are used to stop boats from moving. There are two main types of anchors: temporary and permanent. A permanent anchor is called a mooring block and is not easily moved, according to Wikipedia.

The marriage vows state "till death do us part," which indicates the marriage is permanent. To make sure the marriage is secure, it must be connected to a permanent anchor. When the winds of life blow, an anchor keeps the marriage in place and causes it to stay on course. That anchor should be strong, steady, and secure. If you attempt to make anything other than God your mooring block, it's just a matter of time before your marriage shipwrecks.

~ A MOMENT OF REFLECTION ~

I am grateful that I never encountered physical abuse during my marriage. However, I am aware that many women endure such harsh attacks. I also realize that there are many forms of abuse.

"Who brought me out from my enemies. You also lifted me up above those who rose up against me; You delivered me from the violent man" (2 Samuel 22:49, AMPC).

Abuse is any action or behavior that causes harm or mental anguish. According to marriage.com, there are eight types of abuse: emotional, sexual, physical, intellectual, material and financial, mental, cultural, and discriminatory.

There are many marriages in trouble, and some wives/husbands suffer in silence. According to medium.com, six types of emotional abuse can occur in relationships:

1. Verbal insults and belittling
2. Gaslighting
3. Emotional neglect
4. Control and manipulation
5. Intimidation and threats
6. Blame-shifting and guilt-tripping

If you are in a physically abusive marriage, I suggest you seek shelter somewhere else as soon as possible. Don't think twice about leaving;

devise an exit strategy. Never subject yourself to physical abuse under any circumstances. Remember, nobody loves you more than you.

Do you feel safe and secure? Are you happy? Is there an incredible deep-down hurt that you don't have words to explain? If you are waiting for things to change, it may be a good idea to wait in another location. In many cases, you think things will get better, but they progress from bad to worse.

You should set boundaries because people will treat you the way you allow them to. You must view yourself as valuable and love yourself if you want someone else to. Nobody can defend you like you.

The church is where people turn when they have exhausted all means. They are broken and distraught, seeking help. Situations in life have overwhelmed them, and church should be their haven. The problem is that in many churches, people are just like the world. People go to church and know all the proper protocols. They know how to put their finger up when walking; they know how to single and double clap; they even know the proper places to say amen when the pastor is preaching. But the word of God says:

"Therefore, lay aside all filthiness and overflow of wickedness, and receive with meekness the implanted word, which is able to save your souls. But be doers of the word, and not hearers only, deceiving yourselves. For if anyone is a hearer of the word and not a doer, he is like a man observing his natural face in a mirror; for he observes himself, goes away, and immediately forgets what kind of man he was" (James 1:21-24, NKJV).

Couples put on their Sunday best with smiles on their faces. They are active in church, serving on different auxiliaries. Some even preach from the pulpit. But they can't wait to get in the car; they fuss and even curse each other out. Some men/women physically abuse their spouses and still attend church. If God is a healer, why don't the couples that attend church allow Him to heal their marriages? It's shameful; the church should be throwing out lifelines to rescue lost souls that are looking for help. But in many cases, people in the church need a lifeline themselves. The word of God says in Luke 6:46 (NLT), *"So why do you keep calling me 'Lord, Lord!' when you don't do what I say?"* If we proclaim to be Christians, we should allow the word of God to transform us by renewing our minds with the word of God.

Then we have the Christians that can keep a secret well; that is, their own secret. They want to know everybody else's business but never share the intimate details of their lives. There is no way we can sincerely help others if we don't share how God brought us through situations. 2 Corinthians 1:4 tells us that when we are comforted by God we are to comfort others with the same comfort. Sharing our victories is God's design to help strength our brothers and sisters.

Church should be a safe place, but many people experience unpleasant interactions dealing with church folk. They need help but, due to skepticism, feel they can't be transparent. Let me give you an example: "Please pray for me." "Okay, what is your prayer request?" "I have an unspoken request." The purpose for prayer is agreement, therefore I submit unto you that there is no such thing as an unspoken prayer request. People are reluctant to be open because they don't want to be judged or discussed. Therefore, if you can't reveal the request, it would be better to say, "Pray for me as The Holy Spirit leads; I stand in need of prayer."

The church sets no example when it comes to divorce. When couples made their vows before God expressing both commitment and promise, they made an agreement with each other and entered a holy covenant. Marriage is not 50/50 if the husband spends 100% of his time seeking to please his wife and the wife spends 100% of her time seeking to please her husband. They would both be well pleased. I submit to you that this would be a great teaching in churches!

You have two people from different rearing styles and backgrounds, not to mention two different personalities coming together as one. You will have to learn to compromise to settle issues; it's not just you any longer. Remember, two are now one. If one of you grabs on tight to God's word and trusts Jesus as you ride the waves of life, it will make a tremendous difference in your marriage.

It's wonderful to get married and blend families together. The most effective way to maneuver this type of situation is the husband and wife being of one accord. Don't allow the children to separate you by the wife telling them one thing and the husband another. Remember, your coming together as families should enhance, not divide. The special relationship you have with your children should not end because you decided to get married. The husband/wife should be careful of the spirit of jealousy that could try to arise. Close all doors to the enemy in the beginning, and set boundaries. Remember, when you married each other, your problems also became one. There is no problem that can't be resolved, but you must work together; you are on the same team, and if you have allowed a third team to develop, get rid of it. Communication is the answer, not divorce!

An anchor is a necessity because your marriage will enter choppy waters. You will need something to hold it steady. You will be sailing along fine, then suddenly a storm will come out of clear blue skies. That's where the Transcendence of God's Love will take over. His love surpasses our love. His love can do what our love can't. Because God is Love! If He is not your anchor, He is patiently waiting for you to invite Him into your marriage. He will then direct and guide your marriage according to His word and put it on the path of recovery.

You have tried it your way ... What have your results been? Are you tired of being tired? Are you ready to release it and allow God to work it out? Are you ready to trust God to take control because things are so out of control?

"Are you weary, carrying a heavy burden? Come to me. I will refresh your life, for I am your oasis. Simply join your life with mine. Learn my ways and you'll discover that I'm gentle, humble, and easy to please. You will find refreshment and rest in me. For all that I require of you will be pleasant and easy to bear." (Matthew 11:28-30, TPT).

CAROLYN LEE

~PONDERING MOMENTS~

CHAPTER 5

COMMUNICATION CONNECTION

STAY CONNECTED

According to Google, wedding vows are words of commitment, love, and dedication between two people. The bride and groom exchange their promises to one another with their closest loved ones and friends present as witnesses. A wedding vow is a promise, most often in the form of words, exchanged between two people when they get married.

~ A MOMENT OF REFLECTION ~

When you fail to trust, you automatically pull the disconnect line. Be careful revisiting what was discussed and forgiven. Trust is the foundation of marriage; be quick to repair cracks that try to form. Forgiveness is not forgetting, but it's moving forward, leaving what happened in the past. If you still feel something in your heart, ask yourself if you have truly forgiven. It's not fair to your spouse or yourself to keep bringing it up.

Vows should be honored and not given up on so easily. Endurance is a virtue that must be embraced, but the question is how you embrace it. The Bible says in James 1:5 (NLT), *"If you need wisdom, ask our God, and he will give it to you. He will not rebuke you for asking."* The Bible also says in Matthew 19:26 (NLT), *"Jesus looked at them intently and said, Humanly speaking, it is impossible. But with God everything is possible."*

Communication is vital for a successful marriage. I recall when my husband and I would talk throughout the day and night. We would laugh as we shared so many things. We never ran out of things to say; we felt free to express ourselves. Be careful to keep the communication connected. Check the outlet every now and then to keep it secure. Be observant, and recognize changes in your spouse. Don't ignore small things. When you see something out of the ordinary, address it. Keep the communication connection tight between the two of you.

Maintaining a heart connection is imperative. It is the worst feeling to express yourself to your spouse only to feel they are not hearing your words. Most importantly, they are not hearing your heart. The perspective of the wife is important, and the opinion of the husband is equally important; the problem lies in how you express your viewpoints to each other. Both should be respectful of the other, and it is wise to talk after tempers have calmed down. Remember, Love covers, protects, and refuses to hurt.

The challenges of life began to come for us. Allen was laid off work, and he worked day labor to make ends meet. I continued working, taking care of the children, and attending church. There is a business side to marriage; the lights don't just come on, etc. We put our income together. We didn't divide bills; we created them together. Finances can cause a huge disconnect in marriage, so communication is key. Discuss how the bills will be handled and who will take the lead role if you choose not to settle them together. Every major decision should be discussed so that both of you will know the business of the household. There should be no surprises. Once trust is broken when it relates to finance, it's not easily restored.

COMMUNICATION IS TWO-WAY

According to bibleproject.com, a covenant is a relationship between two partners who make binding promises to each other and work together to reach a common goal. Covenants define obligations and commitments.

~ A MOMENT OF REFLECTION ~

"And He answered and said to them, 'Have you not read that He who made them at the beginning made them male and female, and said, 'For this reason, a man shall leave his father and mother and be joined to his wife, and the two shall become one flesh'? So then, they are no longer two but one flesh. Therefore, what God has joined together, let not man separate." (Matthew 19:4-5, NKJV).

Your marriage and whatever situations arise in it are between yourself and your spouse. When you entered a covenant with your spouse, it did not include a third party. I can't stress enough that anything concerning your marriage should be discussed, and decisions made should be between you and your spouse. Every person is different, therefore every marriage is different. There is no cookie-cutter marriage; sure, you can look at other marriages to get examples, but remember you must seek God when it comes to your personal marriage. Advice from others can often lead you down the wrong path.

Beware, everyone you talk to may not have your best interest at heart. The very thing they tell you not to take, in many cases they are taking much more. There have been cases where a husband and wife have separated, and you find the very person you confided in is now flirting with the spouse. It's up to you to guard your marriage by keeping the third party out.

It is important that you and your spouse develop the way you communicate with each other. There is more than one way to communicate. Nonverbal communication expresses a lot without you saying a word. Your body language and facial expressions can say it all.

Beware of silent treatments. According to Wikipedia.org, silent treatment is the refusal to communicate with someone who is trying to communicate and elicit a response. The only way to resolve a problem is to expose it. Remember, marriage is between two, so don't shut your spouse out and go solo.

Master your emotions; don't speak out of anger. Once words are released, no matter how much you apologize, you can never take those words back. When growing up, I often heard, "Sticks and stones may break my bones, but words will never hurt me." That has never been farther from the truth. Words enter your heart, and you can feel them when they land. Words can cause wounds so deep that only the power of God can heal.

Proverbs 18:21 (TPT) says, "*Your words are so powerful that they will kill or give life, and the talkative person will reap the consequences.*"

WARNING: DON'T OPEN THE DOOR

There is a door right in the middle of your marriage. One side of the door says "Love/Covenant," and the other side says "Temptation/Deception." Affection and communication are the delicate hinges that your marriage hangs on. If you are not careful, the door will be opened to Temptation/Deception caused by affection and communication breakdown. Depending on the temptation, the marriage may not survive. If the husband spends his time loving his wife and making sure she is happy, and the wife spends her time respecting her husband and making sure his needs are met, both would be elated, but when the needs of one or the other spouse are unmet, it leaves room for temptation/deception to creep in. Once the door is open, it's hard to close it.

Every woman wants to know that she is beautiful in her husband's eyes. If you don't give your spouse what they need, someone else will. I met a young man at work who began to compliment me. I would have lunch with him from time to time. To be honest, I enjoyed the attention because it was lacking at home. We would talk on the phone in the evenings because my husband would go out with friends after work. I missed the attention he once gave me. I was honest with this young man, telling him that I was married and had a child, and his response attracted me to him even more. He respected me for telling him, and then he responded that he had everything to gain if I chose to continue to talk to him. I am so grateful to God, He kept me during temptation. This young man was working during summer break from college. I gave my life to the Lord in December 1974. When he returned the following summer and approached me at work, I informed him that I had accepted Jesus as my Savior so I could no longer have lunch or hold conversations with him. If not for the grace of God, those lunches and phone conversations could have gone much further. I can say my husband is the only man I have ever known because God kept me.

~ A MOMENT OF REFLECTION ~

I didn't deny my husband when it came to intimacy. Don't get it twisted, it's not that I always felt like it. But you see, I chose to please God even in that area, so I submitted to my husband. Let me share a secret with you ladies: When you anoint yourself with oil and become one with your husband, stroking his back with the anointing oil on your hands and praying on the inside, this is a powerful strategy in the Spirit realm. The Holy Spirit will intervene, for that is the time when you are truly one.

"With much justifying and enticing argument she persuades him; with the allurements of her lips she leads him [to overcome his conscience and his fears] and forces him along. Suddenly he [yields and] follows her reluctantly like an ox moving to the slaughter, like one in fetters going to the correction [to be given] to a fool or like a dog enticed by food to the muzzle. Till a dart [of passion] pierces and inflames his vitals; then like a bird fluttering straight into the net [he hastens], not knowing that it will cost him his life" (Proverbs 7:21-23, AMPC).

There are men and women waiting to comfort you. They stand on the other side of the door, patiently waiting for it to open. Some people are married themselves and look for needs that are not being met at home. Then there are some that don't want a husband or wife because being with someone else's spouse allows them to have no responsibility.

Reasons that will force the door open to Temptation/Deception:

- Withholding lovemaking
- Feeling controlled
- Neglecting to spend quality time together
- Not feeling secure
- Not feeling understood
- Not feeling respected
- Feeling that you are not needed or wanted
- Not being able to express how you feel
- Not being shown appreciation
- Not being trusted; always being accused
- Excessive complaints, criticism, and name-calling
- Being disrespectful to each other
- Embarrassing your spouse in front of others

It is imperative that you and your spouse agree to keep the door shut and not allow Temptation/Deception any place at all in your marriage.

Amos 3:3 (AMPC) says, *"Do two walk together except they make an appointment and have agreed?"*

~PONDERING MOMENTS~

CHAPTER 6

THE DARKEST STORM

THE CALM BEFORE THE STORM

Calm before the storm: "A quiet or peaceful period before a period during which there is great activity, argument, or difficulty," according to the Cambridge English Dictionary.

"A period of unusual tranquility or stability that seems likely to presage difficult times," per the Oxford Dictionary.

"A lull or temporary period of quiet before a tumultuous event, such as a storm or an episode of excitement, activity, violence etc.," per Dictionary.com.

We welcomed our third child, a baby boy, Allen Gean Lee, II, on Tuesday, October 3, 1978, at 10:55 a.m. We were so excited to finally have a son. My husband went to his mother's house and picked her up, saying, "I HAVE A SON! I HAVE A SON!" She replied, "That's good. Now, can you put me down?" We laughed so hard as we reminisced about the day our son was born. Now our family was complete: Tasha, Kisha, and Allen Jr.

I did everything possible to ensure my children knew the Lord. Every week they learned a new scripture. They participated in Sunday School and learned how to go up and speak in front of the church. Friday choir rehearsal and youth Bible study was a must, and they attended Wednesday mid-week service. I wanted them to understand they should be engaged with God during the week, not just on Sundays. I did not send my children to church, I took them, and I lived all I knew before them as an example of a holy life. But there was a missing piece. We did not worship as a family, as their dad did not participate. I never spoke badly to our children about their father. I taught them to pray, and every day they would each include in their prayers, "God, save our daddy." God had blessed me with three children, and it was my responsibility to train them and direct them in the way of God.

"Behold, children are a heritage from the Lord, the fruit of the womb a reward. As arrows are in the hand of a warrior, so are the children of one's youth" (Psalm 127:3-4, AMPC).

Our lives were calm and peaceful. My husband never interfered with me attending church. I made sure dinner was ready every Sunday before leaving for church. I made sure he could eat whenever he was ready. There were times I would stay home to spend quality time with him, but that was not often. I loved God with all my mind, soul, heart, and strength, and He came first in everything.

My husband was a good provider, and he loved his family. We worked together when it came to the children; picking up report cards and taking the children to school or picking them up was a team effort. Again, the missing piece was him being involved spiritually in their lives.

We had an opportunity to move closer to the children's school. There was a building owned by a lady that attended my church. This was a great opportunity to be able to begin saving for our own home.

I always prayed, trusting God to save my husband and thanking Him for his salvation. We were about to enter a new year after moving into our new apartment. That New Year's Eve I will never forget the Holy Spirit directing me to pray like I had never prayed before. I took authority over the devil; I commanded him to take his hands off my husband's spiritual eyes and ears. My husband was a witness to my lifestyle; he saw my walk with God, yet I had no doubt Allen loved me, and I displayed my love for him. It was my desire that our marriage be complete in God. Deep in my heart, I knew there was hope he could be saved.

~ A MOMENT OF REFLECTION ~

That night, I took authority and prayed according to the word of God. I gave God's word back to Him mixed with faith. I prayed according to these scriptures:

"For the unbelieving husband has been made holy by his believing wife. And the unbelieving wife has been made holy by her believing husband by virtue of his or her sacred union to a believer. Otherwise, the children from this union would be unclean, but in fact, they are holy. But if the unbelieving spouse wants a divorce, then let it be so. In this situation the believing spouse is not bound to the marriage, for God has called us to live in peace. And wives, for all you know you could one day lead your husband to salvation. Or husbands, how do you know for sure that you could not one day lead your wife to salvation?" (1 Corinthians 7:14-16, TPT).

"In the same way, you wives must accept the authority of your husbands. Then, even if some refuse to obey the Good News, your godly lives will speak to them without any words. They will be won over by observing your pure and reverent lives. Don't be concerned about the outward beauty of fancy hairstyles, expensive jewelry, or beautiful clothes. You should clothe yourselves instead with the beauty that comes from within, the unfading beauty of a gentle and quiet spirit, which is so precious to God. This is how the holy women of old made themselves beautiful. They put their trust in God and accepted the authority of their husbands" (I Peter 3:1-5, NLT).

"Assuredly, I say to you, whatever you bind on earth will be bound in heaven, and whatever you loose on earth will be loosed in heaven" (Matthew 18:18, NKJV).

"And I give you the keys of the kingdom of heaven, and whatever you bind on earth will be bound in heaven, and whatever you loose on earth will be loosed in heaven" (Matthew 16:19, NKJV).

"The Lord does not delay and is not tardy or slow about what he promises, according to some people's conception of slowness, but He is long-suffering (extraordinarily patient) toward you, not desiring that any should perish, but that all should turn to repentance" (2 Peter 3:9, AMPC).

"Then Jesus said to the disciples, 'Have faith in God. I tell you the truth, you can say to this mountain, "May you be lifted up and thrown into the sea," and it will happen. But you must really believe it will happen and have no doubt in your heart. I tell you, you can pray for anything, and if you believe that you've received it, it will be yours. But when you are praying, first forgive anyone you are holding a grudge against, so that your Father in heaven will forgive your sins, too.'" (Mark 11:22-25, NLT).

"Behold, all souls are Mine; The soul of the father as well as the soul of the son is Mine; The soul who sins shall die" (Ezekiel 18:4, NKJV).

"And I have other sheep (beside these) that are not of this fold. I must bring and impel those also; and they will listen to My voice and heed My call, and so there will be (they will become) one flock under one Shepherd" (John 10:16, AMPC).

Let me encourage you to write the above scriptures down in a journal or on index cards. Feel free to insert your name and your spouse's name where applicable. You are about to enter spiritual warfare, and you will need the word of God; it's your weapon. The Holy Spirit will lead you to other scriptures as well; these are just a few.

"For though we walk in the flesh, we do not war according to the flesh. For the weapons of our warfare are not carnal but mighty in God for pulling down strongholds, casting down arguments and every high thing that exalts itself against the knowledge of God, bringing every thought into captivity to the obedience of Christ" (2 Corinthians 10:3-5, NKJV).

"Behold! I have given you authority and power to trample upon serpents and scorpions, and (physical and mental strength and ability) over all the power that the enemy (possesses); and nothing shall in any way harm you" (Luke 10:19, AMPC).

A STORM IS BREWING

Signs that a storm is coming: "Large, puffy cumulus clouds. Darkening sky and clouds. Abrupt changes in wind direction. Sudden drop in temperature," per www.thehartford.com.

One night, I had a dream that my husband came home from work on a Friday. He turned his pockets inside out and said, "I have no money." I said, "What do you mean, you have no money? Didn't you get paid today?" He responded, "It's up my nose!"

The dream was so real that when I woke up, I told him what I had dreamed. He replied, "I drink beer, alcohol, and I even smoke a little weed, but I would never do drugs." I just kept saying that it seemed so real. He laughed and said, "You shouldn't go to sleep if you are going to be having dreams like that."

My husband worked in another area on his job and met new friends. I could always reach him when he wasn't home; I had everybody's phone numbers and I also knew their wives. But there was a difference in his attitude, and he began to stay out later than usual. I had no way of contacting him, and our communication was way off. Staying out late turned into staying out for days at a time.

I recall that one night, not knowing where he was, I began to search for information and found a phone number in his pocket. I called the number, and a young lady answered the phone. I explained that I was looking for my husband and I found this number in his pocket.

She then asked me a very disturbing question, "Does your husband do drugs?" I responded no, and she went on to say, "If he's hanging out with so and so, if he's not doing drugs, he will be." I hung up stunned as I thought back on the disturbing dream I had a few weeks prior. I noticed changes in my husband's behavior; there was a shift in the wind. Now, after making this phone call, I could feel the dark clouds closing in. I could sense the storm was uncomfortably close.

~ A MOMENT OF REFLECTION ~

There was a storm brewing, and you could feel the shift in the wind blowing. You could smell the stench of the storm in the air; the atmosphere was changing. The clouds were gathering, the demons were meeting, and I was preparing for warfare. You see, if I just lived with my husband and went to church, and he was pleased to live with me if I didn't bother him, and he didn't bother me, things in the spirit realm would have been fine. But once I stood my ground according to the word of God, using the authority of the name of Jesus, and commanded Satan to take his hands off and release my husband, all hell broke out, and I do mean hell, like demons being released from the very pit.

The Bible tells us whatever we bind on earth will be bound in heaven and whatever we loose on earth will be loosed in heaven. In other words, whatever we allow, God will allow, and whatever we don't allow, God won't allow. The problem is, Christians live beneath their privilege because they don't know what rightfully belongs to them. Many Christians just settle for whatever situation they are living in. If your marriage is not what you desire it to be, take authority in the name of Jesus according to the word of God. It's very important to remind God what he said in his word. When you do, be prepared to stand, because there will be resistance in the spirit realm.

Marriage is an example of Christ and the church. *"As the Scriptures say, 'A man leaves his father and mother and is joined to his wife, and the two are united into one.' This is a great mystery, but it is an illustration of the way Christ and the church are one"* (Ephesians 5:31-32, NLT).

When ministering to women who are experiencing troubled marriages, my question is: Are you willing to fight for your marriage according to the word of God and do it His way, not your way? If you could have fixed it, you would have done so already; evidently your way is not working. You see, cursing them out, giving them a piece of your mind, not cooking, not speaking, withholding sex, turning to alcohol or drugs, or any of the things you fight with in the natural won't work because it's a spiritual battle.

No warfare for marriage is identical, but each can be strategically directed by the Holy Spirit. That's why it is very important to present your body as a living sacrifice holy and acceptable to God. Prayer, fasting, studying God's word, and worship are all necessities. This is the only way to close all passageways to the enemy.

HOLD ON AND REST IN HIM

I had no idea how to prepare for this fast-approaching storm. I am so grateful for God's grace and mercy. His Holy Spirit directed me every step of the way as I entered the darkest spiritual storm I had ever encountered. As I look back, I understand God wants me to share my experiences with you. Perhaps it will strengthen and encourage you during your storm. I'm not telling you it's going to be easy or that you will always feel victorious. But I am telling you the word of God works; He loves you and promises never to leave you.

To ensure you survive the storm, you must prepare before the storm hits. Begin to transfer the word of God from your head to your heart. It is imperative to spend time in worship. This is a powerful weapon. Also, the word says lay aside every weight that will hinder you. Every known sin, habit, or hang-up, ask God to take it from you as you by faith give Him everything that is not pleasing to Him. Make sure your heart is clean and pure before God. Be honest with Him because He already knows you inside and out. Please get rid of your attitude; it will only hinder the process. Ask God to humble you. Allow God to transform you as you stand in faith for your marriage to be transformed.

How badly do you want your marriage? Are you willing to give up any and everything that stands in the way of preventing restoration in your marriage? If so, you will have to fight in the spirit like a hungry dog fights to hold onto a steak that someone is trying to take from him. You will have to have that same tenacity and tell Satan, "You can't have my marriage. I command you to let go in Jesus' name!!"

Use the authority in Luke 10:19; you already have victory. Remember, you don't fight from a place of defeat. Jesus has already given you victory, and your fight is to maintain it and claim everything that is already yours, which includes your marriage! I believe when we pray, we should pray for results! We must take our place of authority in the name of Jesus; the responsibility is on us, not God. The Bible says be it done unto you according to your faith. If you can't see it, you can't have it.

~ A MOMENT OF REFLECTION ~

Be honest with God. He knows all about you anyway, according to Psalm 139:1-6.

Ask God to cleanse your heart, according to Psalm 51:10-12.

Write down scriptures that promise what you are believing God for, according to Matthew 21:21-22 and Mark 11:22-24.

Have faith in God, and diligently seek Him, according to Hebrews 11:6.

Agree with God's word, and say only what the word says, according to Ezekiel 37:1-10 and Proverbs 18:21.

Agree with another believer, according to Matthew 18:19.

Refuse to say anything negative about your husband or your marriage, according to Proverbs 18:21.

Be careful who you share with regarding your husband or your marriage, according to Proverbs 13:3 and Psalms 1:1.

Put ALL your trust in God, no matter how it looks or feels, according to Proverbs 3:5-6, 2 Corinthians 5:7, and James 1:7-8.

Rest in God's word, according to Isaiah 40:31, Philippians 4:6-7, and John 14:27.

RIDING OUT THE STORM

I don't have a clue how to deal with the sickness of drug addiction. But I know exactly how it feels as the wife of a person entangled in this horrific bondage. I know how it feels to be alone in a marriage; for more than 20 years we had always made decisions together. I had no doubt my husband loved me, and I loved him. I felt safe and there was no doubt that he would provide for our family. We were happily married, but that happiness was suddenly shaken.

Just like in my dream, very little if any finances made it home. I recall my husband coming home with a man I had never seen before trying to sell me some encyclopedias. After listing to his presentation, turning to my husband, I asked if he forgot we already had encyclopedias. Every payday there was excuse after excuse. One Friday he said that when he cashed his check, he put the money on top of the car, and when he drove off it went flying away. Or after being gone for three or four days, he brought a copy of an eye bond with someone else name and information on it. He then took a pen and wrote his name on top of theirs to prove he was arrested and that they held him for all those days.

Special days were no longer special holidays, anniversaries, birthdays, etc. With each one, I felt a deep empty disappointment. It came to a point where I could no longer protect our children from knowing something was wrong, and that hurt more than anything. When our oldest daughter graduated high school, my husband did not come home from work to get to her graduation on time. Thankfully, we were able to locate a classmate she could ride with, and she made it right in the nick of time to march in with her class. After graduation, we were stranded in the rain for hours before he finally picked us up. I learned a valuable lesson: Whenever anything important was planned, I knew not to allow him to drive the car.

There were so many times I was stranded at work. I recall one day my husband didn't show up and my very good friend Dorothy, who was also my prayer partner, was taking me home. When I spotted our car, I convinced her to turn around, which she did reluctantly, being upset and afraid for me. She pleaded with me not to get out of the car, but I insisted. I was so upset. The car was parked in front of a pawn shop with my husband in the driver's seat. He didn't notice me until I opened the passenger door and sat in the front seat. He began saying, "Go with Dorothy. I'll see you at home later," but I refused to move. The drug dealer was in the pawn shop, but I didn't care. I felt a rage that I had never felt before. When that man got in the car, I can't recall all that I said, but I do remember asking him if he had room for my husband to live with him. I insisted they drive to a gas station and put gas in the car, then I drove off and left them standing there. All with my friend and prayer partner watching and praying from a distance.

I will never forget the time we didn't have a car at all because my husband gave it to the drug dealer to use to pay off a debt.

The biggest and strongest wind that blew was when the drug dealers told my husband they were coming to kill our family because of a debt he owed them. Hearing this news caused feelings I had never experienced. I began praying and anointing the doors and walls of the apartment with oil and pleading the blood of Jesus. I quoted scripture and claimed God's protection, and I prayed in tongues after praying all I knew in English. I needed to get in agreement with the Holy Spirit. I could hear the downstairs door being kicked in; I recall hearing in my spirit that they would not come into this apartment. I continued to pray. I instructed my daughter to take her newborn baby and go upstairs to the third-floor apartment using the back door.

I could hear footsteps coming up the stairs, and the closer they got, the louder and harder I prayed. Finally, they stopped at the front door. I could hear them pacing. I kept praying and quoting the word of God. They continued pacing, and I continued praying. Then, I could hear the footsteps slowly walking downstairs. I don't know what those men heard or saw, and I don't know how many there were. But one thing I knew for sure was that God promised protection for my family, and I heard the Lord say they will not come into this apartment. Just like for the children of Israel, the death angel passed over our family that night. Hallelujah!! God is more than faithful!!

A few days later, I went downstairs to pay rent, and my oldest daughter insisted on going with me. The owner of the building informed me that I had six months to put my husband out or she would increase the rent. She proceeded to say he was no good and I was stupid because he was never going to change. She continued to say, "I can smell food cooking when he comes in late at night. You are stupid." My daughter interrupted her and said, "God is going to save my daddy, and my mother is not stupid!" My daughter said, "Come on, Mama!" I understood this was her building with her family living there, so she felt endangered. I walked away feeling embarrassed, thinking this lady was a member of my church. I was doing all I knew to stand in faith, trusting God to save my husband. I realized she didn't believe like I did. She would talk down about my situation, calling the pastor, telling him and anybody else that would listen what was happening in my personal life.

I would feel so discouraged walking into church wondering what had been said, while different people would stare. One Sunday, the weight seemed unbearable. I could not open my mouth to praise God. Then, on the inside, I heard a voice say, "I know what Allen has done, and I know what people are saying, but what have I done that you can't praise Me." As I lifted my hands that Sunday and praised God, all the weight was lifted. By faith I prayed, "Father, thank you for saving my husband. I trust You."

During this storm, our oldest daughter Tasha began to seek God with all her heart. God always dealt with her in dreams. She would also have visions; one she shared of her dad sitting in a big black chair, weeping. When she would get out of bed because the weeping woke her up to go into the room where the chair was, he would not be there. Tasha also got a job when she graduated high school to help financially. Her sister and brother were still in high school. Tasha held my arms up and encouraged me. She prayed with me and was a constant reminder that God was going to save her daddy. She would ask him to take her to the store, and while they were alone, she would talk to him and try to get him to realize what he was doing was wrong. Yes, Tasha was the oldest, and she took her role seriously.

Kisha, our second daughter, began dating. She graduated high school and spent a lot of time away from home; this is how she escaped what was going on at home.

Allen Jr. was at a critical age when he needed his dad. I'm thankful for his godparents, Inez and Albert Sams. They instilled values in him, and their daughter Diane was a big sister to him. They also had three sons, Jeffery, Joseph, and Romell. They were older, but he spent lots of time with them.

It appeared this storm was raging out of control. You could feel the intensity of the forces of evil pursuing and hear the whistling of the wind. You could hear the howling as the hounds of hell raged in the spirit realm. It appeared my family would be consumed by this fierce storm. I wanted my husband delivered, but my entire family was at stake. You see, the enemy wants to destroy families. If he can disrupt the covenant of marriage, which represents the covenant between God and the church, he will be accomplishing his goal. To be honest with you, this warfare is not between the enemy and mankind; he's doing everything he can to disrupt God's plan.

I was aware that I was in a spiritual battle! The word of God says, *"Beloved, do not think it strange concerning the fiery trial which is to try you, as though some strange thing has happened to you"* (1 Peter 4:12, NKJV). I had to focus my attention on the enemy and direct all my anger, disappointment, and frustrations not on my husband but on the one who launched this attack. I could not see the chains breaking in the spirit realm. As I look back, I realize that's the reason the attack intensified; the chains were breaking! This storm lasted five years. The number five means grace. God gave me grace to stand on His word, trust Him to do what He said He would do, and not give up!

During the most difficult time of my life, I had to trust God and use every tool available to me. I had to ask God to help me forgive my husband. I had to ask Him to create in me a clean heart and renew the right spirit within me. I had to be honest with God and expose all the ugly feelings and thoughts I had allowed to linger in my mind. I had to bring every thought into the obedience of Christ. I made a choice to release everything that was not like God so that I would not hinder the power of God working in my marriage. I would walk the floor confessing the promises of the word of God out loud with authority. I would give God's word back to Him mixed with faith, reminding Him that His word can't return to Him void; it had to do what it said because He honored His word above His name.

I would go through the apartment anointing everything with oil, and when I did laundry, I applied oil to every piece of clothing. When my husband would come home intoxicated, I would put a drop of blessed oil in his mouth. I would plead the blood of Jesus over our apartment and family. I would confess that my husband was saved, delivered, and set free. I realized my husband had a will, and no matter how much I wanted him delivered, he had to want God for himself. I would pray, "Father, help Allen to want to, want to. Turn his heart toward you, take the blinders off his spiritual eyes, and unstop his spiritual ears. Don't give him any peace until he accepts you." I would pray, "Send labors across his path wherever he goes; whatever he does, let someone tell him about Jesus." I would declare that my husband loves God with his whole heart, and every yolk of bondage is broken and destroyed over Him.

I would call His name and pray in tongues because I realized there were things happening in the spiritual realm that I was not aware of, but the Holy Spirit was fully aware. I declared that I am not moved by what I see or how I feel because it is temporal and subject to change. I would bind everything that was not like God; I would name them one by one. I would lose love and contentment in our home. I decreed and declared salvation for my entire household. I would speak directly to Satan and command him to release my husband in Jesus' name. I would pray according to Luke 10:19, standing in the authority given to me. I refused to be moved! God had blessed me with my family, and the devil in hell could not have them! You may say I went to the extreme, but I was in a desperate situation, and I don't care what anyone thinks. I did what God instructed me to do, and I pray you do the same.

Right amid this storm, I was permitted by missionary Idellar Sams to start a women's ministry at church. God would give me messages to minister to hurting women. I could connect with them because I was hurting too. Many women suffer in silence. Their faces are made up, hair done, and outfits sharp, but on the inside, they are broken. The anointing and power of God would manifest in every meeting. I was determined to walk by faith, not by sight. I continued to serve as Vice President of the Nurses' Board and Sunday school teacher and to participate as a licensed missionary. I was doing everything God required of me. I refused to allow doubt to linger. It made many attempts, but I made a choice to resist the devil, and he had to flee.

With all my heart, I believed God would deliver my husband. I knew deep within he wanted to be free. When someone is bound, they can't set themselves free. God is looking for intercessors, someone who will stand in the gap and make up the hedge. For God to work on the earth, He needs a body, which explains why Jesus had a body and God's plan was fulfilled through Him. The word of God said it would be done unto me according to my faith. I was at a point where it did not matter what anyone thought. This was my marriage, and I was determined to hang in there until I got a manifestation. Yes, the storm was still raging, but I was still standing in expectation, in faith according to God's word.

~ A MOMENT OF REFLECTION ~

The word of God says, *"Write the vision and make it plain"* (Habakkuk 2:2, KJV). Find the promises in God's word relating to your marriage, and based upon the word, write what you desire God to do in your marriage. Beware of praying in doubt, for example, "If it be Your will, God, save my husband and heal our marriage." You already know it's His will because He said it in His word. The word plainly says, *"but is longsuffering to us-ward, not willing that any should perish, but that all should come to repentance"* (2 Peter 3:9b, KJV). It also says, *"What therefore God hath joined together, let not man put asunder"* (Matthew 19:6, KJV).

God desires your husband to be saved and your marriage to be healed. You must see it done by faith; if you can't see it, you can't have it. Once you write your vision, don't change your confession, as the word says it may be delayed, but wait for it and don't give up! I can't promise it will manifest in a month or two, but I promise if the words that come out your mouth agree with God's word, it will come to pass. Because God said His word won't return to Him empty. He didn't assign an angel to watch over His word; He watches over it Himself. Remember, God is not like man. If He promised you something, He won't change His mind.

One of the most effective manipulations Satan uses against the body of Christ is unforgiveness. Satan knows that unforgiveness will block your receiving from God. All your prayers, fasting, and confessions will be in vain. Unforgiveness is when we choose not to have compassion for someone that has wronged us. The key is we choose; God has set His principles before us in His word, and we must do it His way, not ours. God is aware of every deep hurt that you can't even put into words. He knows the pain is so deep at times it's hard to function. Your heavenly Father sees you at night with the tears wetting the pillow and you turning it to the other side to find a dry spot. I know personally because I have been where you are. You must be honest with God. Tell Him you need His help to forgive and release your spouse. Tell your heavenly Father you choose to forgive by faith!

Pick your head up! It's not over. Jesus declared, *"It is finished!"* (John 19:30b NKJV). You are in a win, win situation Satan has no winning qualities in him because Jesus defeated him and stripped him of all authority over you!

Don't coward down; stand up! I speak strength and courage to you right now in the name of Jesus. Rise up in your faith! Rise up using the word of God, which is your only effective weapon! Speak the word out of your mouth! Get your oil and anoint your home! Open the door and command every spirit that is not like God to GO! in The Name of JESUS.

~PONDERING MOMENTS~

CHAPTER 7

ANGELS OF ENCOURAGEMENT

God promised never to leave or forsake me, and He is more than faithful! I would not exchange my walk with God for anything. Looking back, I recognize special assigned angels that surrounded me during the most difficult time of my life. I am reminded of Aaron and Hur standing on each side of Moses, holding up his hands. While Moses held up his hands, the Israelites were winning the battle, but whenever he lowered his hands, the enemy would begin winning. I don't have words to express my gratitude for the many angels God assigned to me during this horrific time in my life.

I met Sharon Williams at the bus stop while going to school one morning. I had never seen her before, although we lived on the same block. Sharon and I would go to school together and we would go to lunch together. Sharon and I became best friends, and she was my biggest support during my pregnancy. Sharon and I have always been there for each other during the most difficult times in our lives. I was married first. We laugh as we reminisce because I married a guy named

Allen. She married a guy named Allen. I had a son, Allen Jr. She had a son, Little Allen. I always teased her, saying she wanted to be just like me. The Lord blessed me and my husband with three children: LaTasha, Dekisha, and Allen Jr. Sharon and her husband were blessed with two sons, Little Allen and William. I was her children's godmother, and she was my children's. Sharon's mother and father became my godparents, and her sisters and brother became my siblings. My children would wake up on some Christmas mornings at her house. When I attended my parents' funerals, my children were at my best friend's house. We made it a tradition to spend every New Year's Day together. Sharon was my rock during the most trying times of my life. She was there financially, a great support and encouragement. I could share exactly how I felt because we knew each other, and we always shared without reservation. Sharon was there for the children in any way she could be. She was and still is one of my special angels, My Best Friend. I love and appreciate our special friendship.

I was chasing my son one Sunday morning at church; he did more running than walking. We ran right past Dorothy Mathews, who was standing there with her little girl, Tiffany. I turned and said to Dorothy, "What's wrong with him?" She replied, "He's just being a boy." We chuckled. You see, I had two little princesses, so I had to learn how to deal with a prince. Weeks later, the Lord placed it on my heart to ask Dorothy if she wanted to be prayer partners. We began praying and reading the word every morning. We received many answers as we petitioned God for so many situations. God showed Himself strong in many areas of our lives and in our families. We trusted God for our children; we prayed them through some very trying times from childhood to adulthood. We will never cease praying for our husbands, children, grandchildren, great-grandchildren, and as far as our bloodlines extend. Our children mention from time to time that they can remember hearing us calling their names in prayer. This test with my marriage was one of the biggest mountains we faced during all the years we prayed together. It was a five-year long haul, and Dorothy was there every step of the way. She prayed with me, cried with me, and encouraged me. She often expressed having a difficult time watching me go through this fiery trial. She supported me financially and emotionally while I stood in faith.

Dorothy would say, "Carolyn, I agree with what you want God to do, but I'm not sure if I could go through this test like you." Dorothy and I have a special connection, and when we pray and study the word, God always manifests Himself to us. We can talk to each other about anything, and we are very careful to take all our conversations to God in prayer. I'm grateful God had the perfect prayer partner for me; we've learned so much from each other and have witnessed God expand our spiritual territories. Dorothy and I have prayed together for more than 44 years. Dorothy is my prayer partner, sister in Christ, friend, confidant, and my forever angel.

My mother's name was Miley. She had five brothers, Ben, John, James, Henry, and Alonzo, and two sisters, Sophie and Maude. Aunt Sophie had a daughter named Yvonne; we had a special relationship as we spent a lot of time together growing up. Aunt Maude had a daughter named Dollie. We did not spend much time together growing up. We developed a relationship after I accepted Jesus, when we became very close and did everything together. Doll became my sister, friend, and confidant. We communicated every day. Doll joined the same church I attended, and I witnessed God work miracles in her body. She had two beautiful children, Lisa and Katrina. After marrying Fredrick Shelton, she had a deep desire to have children with him. God healed her of female issues and opened her womb, and she gave birth to two more beautiful daughters, Ebonie and Monica.

Doll and I were expecting babies at the same time, and we would pray over the babies in our wombs every day. At that time, they didn't do ultrasounds, so there was no gender reveal until the baby was born. But Doll and I had a plan. We were both going to have boys, Allen Jr. and Fred Jr. They were going to grow up together. Allen Jr. was born October 3, 1978. Doll called me to agree in prayer that all would go well before she went to the hospital to deliver her baby. She called me the next morning, November 11, 1978, to tell me she had a healthy baby girl. I was so disappointed, but we concluded the baby was healthy, and this must be God's plan. Fred named the baby Ebonie. Doll asked me to give the baby her middle name, Shanea. Allen Jr. and Ebonie were extremely close. Allen Jr. always referred to her as "my Ebonie." This is a very short glimpse of my angel Doll and our special relationship.

When I was in the Darkest Storm of my life, expecting a miracle in my marriage, Doll was right there. She undergirded me both spiritually and naturally. Doll stood on the word of God with me without wavering. I recall her saying, "Carolyn, do you really believe, because I do." I just smiled and said, "Yes, Doll, I really believe God." When my grandmother passed away, I was emotional and unable to drive; she was another mother. This is the time you need your spouse, but at that time I had no idea where my husband was. I will be forever grateful for my cousin Doll who drove me and my children to the service and cemetery. She prayed the whole time.

Another incident I will never forget is the night the landlord told me that my husband had another woman. She volunteered to take me to a bar where they were known to hang out. When I told Doll, she begged me not to go because it was in the middle of the night. She made me promise to call her when I got home. She was so relieved when I let her know I was home; she had been praying the whole time. We sat outside this lounge for hours, but I never saw my husband or another woman. To this day, I have never had proof of another woman. Now, don't get me wrong, I know things happen, but I never had any proof of a relationship other than the one he had with drugs.

Ebonie suffered an asthma attack just before her baby was born. Both her and the baby were deprived of oxygen. Doll and I would pray day and night, expecting a miracle, but Ebonie transitioned in January 1999. We concluded that after we had done all to trust God, we had to submit to His will. My cousin's daughter was gone, and all she had left behind was a baby with severe brain damage. Doll and I continued to pray, but this was more than she could bear. Four months later, Doll transitioned, in May 1999. She would say to me, "Carolyn, I don't understand, but I'm trying not to let it get to my heart." I believe she died of a broken heart, but one thing's for sure, she now has all her answers. Five months later, in October 1999, our precious angel Brizhae joined her mother and grandmother. I'll never forget my last conversation with Doll. She asked, "Carolyn, do you think Allen is saved for real, because you have been through enough?" I had a difficult time releasing Doll, but I take comfort knowing we will one day praise God together around His throne. My angel Doll is always with me in my heart, and I have no doubt that she is looking out for me.

I will never forget my angel Helen Dockery-Hudson, who lived on the second floor of the apartment building we lived in. One night at about 1 a.m., Helen came to our apartment. She asked if I could come to her apartment. I was feeding our daughter Kisha, who was a few weeks old and always woke up about that time. Helen shared a disturbing dream she had of a bus; everybody on the bus was wearing white, and the driver would not let her on because she was not wearing the right clothes. That night, Helen accepted Jesus as her Lord and Savior, and I was honored to help her get dressed!

Helen was right there when my mother transitioned. I trusted her to keep my children. She fell in love with Kisha and became her second godmother.

Helen was a witness to the turmoil in my marriage. I will never forget when she found out the drug dealer was threating to kick the door in and kill the whole family. Helen was livid. She said, "Carolyn, throw Allen out!! When Jonah was running from God and got on that boat and the sea was in an uproar, when they found out Jonah was causing the problem, they threw him overboard. I know you want God to save him, but he doesn't have to be there in the house with you and the kids for God to do that." Helen prayed with me, cried with me, and was a great encouragement. Before Helen transitioned, Allen and I were at her bedside. I was so grateful that she had on the right clothes and God had allowed me to help her get dressed. I'm also grateful she got a chance to witness the Miracle of Allen's salvation. I have no doubt Helen is watching out for me; she will always be my angel.

My sister Ora was my special night angel; she would listen, cry, and pray with me during the midnight hours, the darkest part of the night. My older sister is still my angel!

Lorraine Render and Charlene Johnson were two special angels God had stationed at work. We would pray in the spirit, fast, and read God's word, turning the conference room into a prayer room. Glory to God, lunchtime became warfare time! We would pray that God would give me strength and that God would send people to witness to my husband. Lorraine and Charlene encouraged me and were a financial blessing to me during some very dark days. They are still two of my wonderful angels.

I have no doubt that Dorothy Adams is singing in the heavenly choir. While I was standing in faith, Dorothy would call me and sing, "My soul has been anchored in the Lord." Then, she would come by and give me money to buy food. Yes, Dorothy was a very special angel in my life, and I am so grateful God placed her in my life.

My godparents Canary and Tommie Williams were very important angels in our lives. It was years before my children found out they were not their biological grandparents. But that didn't change a thing; they loved my children as if they were their own flesh and blood. They were sent by God to fill a void in their lives. We celebrated many New Year's Days together. My God Dad would always say, "Happy New You." I have no doubt my God Dad Tommie is watching over us from heaven.

Pastor Willie Sams was the one whom my mother entrusted me to before she transitioned. Pastor Sams was a personal guardian angel as well my spiritual father. Pastor Sams is the one who saw the gift of teaching God placed upon my life. I'll never forget my first message, "Major in Holiness." Pastor Sams encouraged me to bring that message and countless more. Pastor Sams was very instrumental during my formulative years as a Christian. I will be forever grateful for the late Sister Elnora Sams. I will never forget her keeping the children when they were ill so that I could continue to work. She shared the wisdom of a mother with me as we enjoyed many Monday dinners together. She is now in heaven and will always be my angel.

God blessed me with two angels Inez and Albert Sams. I am forever grateful for them allowing us to be part of their family. They were a second set of godparents to my son, and as a result, they became my godparents as well. Our families became intertwined, and we have wonderful fellowship together. Inez was there during some of the darkest times of my life. They will always hold a special place in my heart!

Mother Susie Clark was another angel assigned to me. Our children attended a school across the street from her house, and she allowed our children to go to school from her home. She was another godmother to me and was a blessing and encouragement in many ways. I will forever cherish our conversations and her words of wisdom. I have no doubt Mother Clark is watching over me from heaven.

Missionary Idellar Sams was the angel that led me in the prayer of salvation. She had a comforting, gentle voice. I recall her words, "I know you are tired, but don't give up. God is going to save your husband. Let me share something with you. There was a lady who was saved, but her husband was a heavy drinker. After praying for his salvation for many years, she grew tired. The lady divorced him, and a few years later, the man got saved and remarried. The new wife received all the benefits of her prayers. Don't give up! God is going to save your husband!" Missionary Idellar Sams will always be one of my special angels as she cheers me on from heaven.

"For He shall give His angels charge over you, to keep you in all your ways" (Psalm 91:11, NKJV).

"The angel of the Lord encamps all around those who fear Him and delivers them" (Psalm 34:7, NKJV).

TRANSCENDENT LOVE

~PONDERING MOMENTS~

CHAPTER 8

WHEN THE END IS THE BEGINNING

But those who wait on the Lord shall renew their strength; They shall mount up with wings like eagles, they shall run and not be weary, they shall walk and not faint" (Isaiah 40:31, NKJV).

"Fear not, for I am with you; Be not dismayed, for I am your God. I will strengthen you, Yes, I will help you, I will uphold you with My righteous right hand" (Isaiah 41:10, NKJV).

"For I know the thoughts that I think toward you, says the Lord, thoughts of peace and not of evil, to give you a future and a hope" (Jeremiah 29:11, NKJV).

NOTHING HAPPENS BY CHANCE

We were at the end of our lease. It had been five long, agonizing years, and it was time to move. I was looking for an apartment on the West Side of Chicago; that's the only area I had ever lived in. Our daughter Tasha mentioned to one of her friends that we were looking for an apartment. This friend had an aunt who knew a lady on the South Side of Chicago that wanted to rent her house. She gave my daughter this lady's phone number, and I gave her a call out of courtesy, explaining to her that I had never lived on the South Side and didn't plan on moving south. The lady encouraged me, saying it wouldn't hurt to come and look at the house, so my husband and I went to see the house. I can't explain it, but I knew it was the right thing to do. There is no doubt God was directing my path every step of the way. We moved to the South Side, and I began visiting a church that I had been invited to by my friend Charlene Johnson.

On December 27, 1996, my husband was not home. I was up praying late in the midnight hour when the Lord began speaking to me:

"You want your husband set free, then Carolyn, you must obey Me. When I prompt you to pray, make haste and do it right away. For this battle, I'll fight for you, but to seek Me and pray is what I want you to do. Don't slack up or take it with ease, for it's consistency, you see. I've brought you this far, and I won't leave you now. The devil would have you think he's in charge somehow. But you know that can't be because he's been whipped and has no victory. For you will see this thing completely unfold before your eyes. It won't be much longer, and you know I can't lie. Just continue to trust in Me and you will see I have given you the victory. Yes, you two shall walk hand in hand; for you that is my plan, and I will use you in ministry to bring other men and women to Me. Trust in Me and don't doubt, for I will surely bring it about. The poetry you see will also be a part of that ministry. For the poems will begin to unfold with messages that have yet to be told, and many people they will reach as through the poetry you will teach. The experiences you've had will put you in touch with the hearts of many, and the hurt is much. For you will comfort and show them how to stand. Many women will be encouraged by your hand. Don't you see, Carolyn Lee, I have great plans for thee!"

One morning, my daughter Kisha and I were getting ready for work. My husband had not come home the night before with the car, which left us with no way to get to work. I called my cousin Johnny Johnson and asked if we could get a ride with him and his wife Gwen. My cousin lived a few blocks away, and he and his wife were there for us during this dark time in our lives. I will be forever grateful for their love and support. My husband came home before my cousin arrived.

I will always remember this special morning. With my husband sitting on the bed, I said, "Enough is enough. I love you enough to release you to live your life the way you want to." You see, I felt I had put my husband in God's hands, but on this morning, I was totally releasing him. I continued, "I have been a wife to you despite all the pain you have caused our family. I have prayed and cried; I have fasted and trusted God to save you, but enough is enough. This evening when I come home, have all your clothes packed, and I will drop you off wherever you want to go. If you ever decide you want to be a responsible husband and father, call me, and I will pick you up. I still trust God to save you, but you don't have to be in this house for Him to do that."

I walked out of the bedroom. I could hear my husband weeping, but to be honest, I didn't care. He hadn't cared about my tears all these years. But then, I heard God on the inside of me saying, "Go back and minister to him, not as your husband but minister to him as you would to another soul." When I went back into the bedroom, he was no longer sitting on the bed but had slid onto the floor, sobbing. You see, my husband had been a fighter all his life, but he was not able fight this strong hold. My husband was accustomed to fighting in the natural world, but this was a spiritual battle. With humility and gentleness, I asked, "Are you ready to try God? You have tried it your way and it has not worked." He replied, "I pray, but God don't hear me." I responded, "If you sincerely repent, God will hear you." Then I said, "Allen, would you like to accept Jesus as your personal Lord and Savior?" He said "Yes." All Glory Be to God!! That morning, by God's Grace, my husband repeated the words after me, repenting of his sins and asking Jesus to come into his heart to be his Lord and Savior.

I knew just saying a prayer was not enough. God directed me with His wisdom. I asked our daughter Kisha to come into the bedroom. I said, "Your daddy just accepted Jesus as his personal Savior and Lord, didn't you, Allen?" He replied, "Yes." I continued, "And your dad will be going to church with us, right, Allen?" He replied, "Yes." I went on to say, "If you change your mind about going to church, you can no longer stay in this house." Still weeping, he agreed. You see, I knew being in a place where he could receive the word was the only way he could grow in God. As a family, we became members of Abundant Life Teaching Center under the leadership of the late Pastor James E. Watson. My friend Charlene said the Lord placed in her heart to sow $3.00 into my husband every Sunday; she instructed him to give $1.00 to Sunday School and $2.00 to church offering. By doing this, she planted a seed that remains to this day. Allen never goes to church without a seed to sow.

DON'T BE MOVED BY WHAT YOU SEE

"Since we consider and look not to the things that are seen but to the things that are unseen: for the things that are visible are temporal (brief and fleeting), but the things that are invisible are deathless and everlasting" (2 Corinthians 4:18, AMPC).

I dreamed one night that a snake was about to bite me in the face. I woke up saying the blood of Jesus and praying; the dream seemed so real. One Saturday evening, my husband came home from visiting his mother. At this time, we agreed he would not drive because he was not strong enough to resist the temptations; he was still struggling with habits. On this evening, he came home demanding the keys to the car, saying he was going to the West Side, and I couldn't stop him. When I refused, he began screaming, out of control, then he lifted his hand and drew it back to hit me. The memory of the dream came rushing back. I began to quote Luke 10:19, stomping my feet, marching back and forth, saying "Behold, God has given me authority to trample on serpents and scorpions, and over all the power of the enemy and nothing shall by any means hurt me."

I said this repeatedly as loud as I could, and my husband began to back up; eventually, he went to the basement. The next morning, he didn't remember anything, and he said he had a bad hangover. His stepfather made moonshine; he drank too much of it. I didn't know what he did or what happened. All I knew was God's word is true and cannot lie, and I trust His word.

You see, when a person repents of their sins and invites Jesus to come into their heart, that's only the first step. My husband sincerely repented, and when he did, the Holy Spirit placed him into the body of Jesus Christ and took residence in his spirit, which had been dead. He was then born again in his spirit. But his soul was where he made all his decisions all his life, where his will and emotions were, and where the flesh nature lived and was in control of everything he did. The Holy Spirit had not taken residence in his soul. That's why going to church was so important; he could receive the word of God and be transformed in his mind and learn how to walk in the spirit, and he could then learn to allow the Holy Spirit to live in his soul and not just in his spirit. As he practiced walking in the spirit, the actions of his body would also change. You see, God does not want to be God of your spirit only but of your spirit, soul, and body.

"Now may the God of peace Himself sanctify you completely; and may your whole spirit, soul, and body be preserved blameless at the coming of our Lord Jesus Christ. He who calls you is faithful, who also will do it" (1 Thessalonians 5:23-24, NKJV).

"I beseech you therefore, brethren, by the mercies of God, that you present your bodies a living sacrifice, holy, acceptable to God, which is your reasonable service. And do not be conformed to this world, but be transformed by the renewing of your mind, that you may prove what is that good and acceptable and perfect will of God" (Romans 12:1-2, NKJV).

On Wednesday nights during mid-week service, the women and men would separate for teaching time and then reassemble for service. One

Wednesday, Pastor Walter Dean approached me and said, "God did something for your husband tonight." When I saw Allen, he was wet with sweat and breathing hard. He said, "I'm so tired, and I feel raw inside from my throat to my stomach." He went on to tell me what happened. "Pastor Dean said lift your hands and worship; all the men lifted their hands, and as I closed my eyes and began to worship, I could feel something pushing me in my back down onto the floor. Then I started saying words I did not understand. I tried to stop talking, but I couldn't, then I was on my stomach flat on the floor. I could not stop speaking whatever I was saying. In my mind, I was thinking what's wrong with me? Am I going crazy? But the speaking continued, and from my throat to my belly the sound came out like what felt like forever. When it lifted and I got up, I noticed the same thing had happened to another young man next to me; we had the same experience."

All Glory and Honor be to The King of Kings and the Lord of Lords!!! God is more than faithful! God completely delivered my husband and filled him with the Holy Spirit! If we can believe His word, He will do what His word says!

God set my husband totally free! He threw his cigarettes out, and his desire for cocaine, alcohol, and weed were gone with no withdrawals! The desires that lived in his soul and controlled his body had been evicted, and the Holy Spirit took up residence. Glory be to God!!

~ A MOMENT OF REFLECTION ~

When we are standing in the gap praying and believing God's word, we will experience resistance in the spirit realm because we are in a spiritual battle. The enemy knows he is defeated, and he can't stop our husbands from being delivered, so he attempts to get us to stop their deliverance. He does this by planting thoughts in our minds. If we allow the thoughts to stay in our minds, they will take root in our hearts. Once that thought gets lodged in your heart, you have lost the battle.

NEVER change your confession! I don't care what happens, how you feel, or how bad it looks, the key is to keep the word of God coming out of your mouth. Say what you want to see, not what you see. We would go to my mother-in-law's house, and she would be talking about the horrible things my husband was doing and how disappointed she was in him. I would respond, "Mrs. Lee, God is going to save Allen." I would meet my sister-in-law Lucille, who was married to my husband's brother Payton, and having lunch she would ask about my husband. We would discuss some things, but I never left her presence without telling her, "God is going to save Allen." Lue would always say, "You think so?" and I would respond, "I know so."

I can't express the joy I felt to take my saved and delivered husband to the church where the landlord had said he would never be anything. There was a celebration, and I had been invited. This landlord was in attendance. As I entered the church, I could still hear the words that she said to me: "You're stupid. He is never going to change." Yes, I came face to face with the landlord who went up on my rent because I wouldn't put my husband out. My husband shared that this landlord would come to our apartment in her negligee after I had gone to work and knock on the door, saying she needed to discuss something with him. He would reply, "My wife is at work, and I have to go to work in a few hours," and then he would close the door.

Learn the lessons from this test. Go through the process, and you will experience an awesome testimony. Hang in there, and don't give up. What you are experiencing will help someone else down the road. God has a way of taking our mess and making a message out of it. The lemons you were served that made your mouth pucker, God will show you the right amount of water and sugar to add so that someone else can be refreshed.

Let me encourage you to yield to God as He molds, makes, and shapes you to be the vessel He can use to deliver someone else. This test and trial will come to an end, and you will come out victorious in Jesus' name!

~PONDERING MOMENTS~

CHAPTER 9

STARTING OVER

LEARNING TO TRUST AGAIN

When trauma has been inflicted upon a marriage, trust must be regained. I had to learn to trust my husband again. God had delivered my husband, and now I had to allow Him to do a work inside of me. I had gotten accustomed to overseeing everything. I didn't have to ask his opinion about anything because he was not there. I was the one who drove the car; therefore, I made all the decisions about the car and everything else. I was the one that handled the money because in the past he blew it all. I had to pray and ask God to help me to find my lane and stay in it. I had to relinquish control and give it to my husband.

To be honest, it was one of the hardest things I ever had to do. My husband was the head, but when the head malfunctioned, I was forced to step up and take control. I took the position as head, getting directions from God; therefore, it wasn't easy to give control back to my husband, who in God's order is the head of the woman.

"But I want you to know that the head of every man is Christ, the head of woman is man, and the head of Christ is God" (1 Corinthians 11:3, NKJV).

When your heart has been broken repeatedly for five years, it takes the power of God to heal it. Only God can restore the blood flow to the ventricle and arteries. Forgiveness is the key to healing; you must release all the hurts of the past and embrace the forgiveness and love of God. We must forgive by faith. Just as God forgave us and had compassion on us, we should do the same for others.

"He will again have compassion on us and will subdue our iniquities. You will cast all our sins into the depths of the sea" (Micah 7:19, NKJV).

Love must be rekindled. When the winds of life blow, they cause the flames to get low. We had to work at fanning the flame by dating again, and I must admit I enjoyed being courted. The love was still there, but it needed some tender loving care. Now we were able to experience the things of God together. This relationship was new; it was like I had a new husband. I have heard women say this is my second or even third marriage. That's exactly how I felt. I had a new husband in the same body, and I was falling in love all over again.

I had been active in my previous church, but the Lord directed me to sit and learn alongside my husband. In 1996, as a family we became members of Abundant Life Teaching Center under the leadership of the late Pastor James E. Watson. My husband and I attended the new members classes and teacher training classes together. We joined the prison ministry in 1997. We endeavored to be faithful to God in everything, including in our tithe and offering. And our gifts made room for us. When we first started going to the prison, there was a group of people, but after a while there were only my husband, myself, and the late Chaplain-Pastor James Anderson remaining. Under Chaplain Anderson's training and mentorship, my husband and I ministered at Cook County Correction Penal Institution two times a month. We also ministered at the Juvenile Correctional Facility once a month.

God expanded our territory, and the doors were opened for us to minister at the Federal Penitentiary in downtown Chicago. God saw fit to expand our territory further and open doors at Pontiac and Sheridan Penal Institutions. We ministered under the leadership of the late Bishop DeArmond Mathews. After Bishop Mathews transitioned, we continued ministering and were ordained Pastors of Jehovah Jireh Outreach Ministries Int'l. under the leadership of Apostle Rhonda Mathews. All of this was the fulfillment of what God spoke to me on December 27, 1996, "You two shall walk hand in hand; for you that is my plan, and I will use you in ministry to bring other men and women to Me. Trust in Me and don't doubt, for I will surely bring it about."

During the prison ministry services, Allen was able to share his testimony of how God delivered him. He could relate to those people because he had been where they were. He would embrace and greet every man as they entered the room and embrace and encourage them as they left. Allen would minister the word of God to the men, and I would minister to the women. By the guidance of The Holy Spirt, I would invite them to receive Christ in their hearts. We won't know until we get to heaven how many souls were saved through the Prison Ministry. April 17, 2018, God rewarded our faithfulness at Sheridan Correctional Penal Institution; we received awards for Volunteers of the Year. We reverently placed ALL honor and accolades and every thank you at the feet of our Lord and Savior Jesus Christ; to Him alone be ALL Glory, Honor and Praise.

PROMOTIONS COME FROM ABOVE

My husband and I endeavored to be faithful to God; many times it was a sacrifice. Praise God; He is our provider!

I recall traveling 1 hour 23 minutes, 85.7 miles, to minister at Pontiac Correctional Center with little money. It was a rainy day, and when leaving the facility, we saw two ladies walking. My husband stopped and asked if he could drop them off someplace. The ladies stated they were going to the train, so he invited them into the car out of the rain. My husband suggested that since we were headed toward Chicago maybe he could drop them off at a bus stop near their destination. They responded that if we could take them to Cicero Ave, right off I55, they could take a bus from there. My husband agreed. When we arrived at the gas station, one of the ladies put $50 in my husband's hand. When you take care of God's business, He will take care of yours.

In 2008, My husband and I were licensed as ministers at the Word Made Flesh Ministries under the leadership of Apostle James and Pastor Michelle Ford. In 2010, my husband and I received training and certification at Prison Fellowship Ministries under the leadership of Field Director Mary Johnson. On June 18, 2011, my husband and I graduated and received certification in Biblical Studies and were licensed as Ministers of the Gospel at Trinity Christian Bible Institute under the leadership of Dr. Andrena Lane Trotter.

In March 2014, my husband and I were ordained as Associate Pastors of New Life Outreach World Changing Ministries. It is a privilege and honor to be co-laborers with Pastor Ronnie and Lady Ruth Woodfork. My husband is also a member of the Governing Board, and I serve as Director of Christian Education. Also, in March 2014, my husband and I were appointed and ordained Pastors of Jehovah Jireh Outreach Ministries Int'l under the leadership of Apostle Rhonda Mathews.

After hosting personal Bible studies for several years with additional requests, I was directed by the Holy Spirit to expand further by adding a 4 p.m. Tuesday Bible study, which began February 6, 2024.

On March 3, 2024, God expanded my territory, utilizing James and Lorraine Render, owners of WJWR Internet Radio. I became the Host of Inspiration from Above Radio Broadcast, where the goal is to impart Inspiration-Revelation and Motivation. The program airs on Sundays at 7:30 a.m. and again at 12:30 p.m.

My husband says to me, "I fell into a trap. When offered crack cocaine, I would refuse it. I felt I was strong enough to hang out with this crowd and not participate. Finally, I said let me see what this is like. Instantly, I was trapped. Carolyn, God had a plan from the very beginning. He knew when I met you that you would direct me to Him. God knew I needed to know Him. I wasn't raised in church. Without you praying for me, I would be dead naturally and spiritually. Everybody else had given up on me, but you refused to let go. I'm grateful that you are my wife. Thank you. I love you." My response to him is always, "Sweetheart, I love you too." To God be ALL the Glory!

~PONDERING MOMENTS~

CHAPTER 10

LOVE CONQUERS ALL

THE GREATEST LOVE STORY EVER TOLD

When we read the Bible, we witness a love that transcends time, barriers, and all principalities and powers. It is demonstrated in a way that can't be denied. God exhibited the first show and tell of how to operate in love. God is love. There is nothing else that can flow out of him. God created us in his image and in his likeness; therefore, if we are birthed from God, we are birthed in love. The transcendent love of God should be flowing from our inner man, which is the spirit of God residing in us. This powerful love should flow in every part of our lives, and when it doesn't, we are allowing the flesh nature to hinder that flow. When we accept Jesus into our hearts, God gives us a new nature; that's why we are born again. But the old nature is always there; we must submit to the spirit nature.

TRANSCENDENT LOVE

Our heavenly Father has a love so deep for us it transcended every obstacle to reach everyone. I am forever grateful for the strategies He released on behalf of our marriage. When my husband was entangled in the bondage of drugs and alcohol, God demonstrated His love through me. The only way I was able to stand during this horrific time was because of the transcendent love of God directing me every step of the way.

I've had people say to me, "You are so strong; I don't think I could have passed this test the way you did." ALL Glory to God! The Holy Spirit did ALL the work. Let me share a secret with you. The only thing I can take credit for is yielding to God completely; you see, God wants all of us. I would pray and tell God I want everything He has for me and according to His word. I believed with all my heart that God wanted my marriage whole. I was willing to do things God's way, according to His word. I had to allow the transcendent love of God to flow in every area of my being. Glory be to God. His love flowed through hurt, tears, disappointments, fears, and the biggest hurdle: unforgiveness. I felt like every time I tried to forgive, I was kicked again in the same wound. I made a choice to allow God to forgive and love my husband through me. Because I was obedient to God, He healed my broken heart, which resulted in Him being Glorified!

The greatest love story that has ever been told is God's transcendent love for us. Our heavenly Father loved us with a love so great there are no words to express it, yet we turned our backs on Him. But He never stopped pursuing us. Every new day that He allows us to wake up and go about our daily lives, He extends His generous grace, mercy, and love. Many people take what they need out of God's hand then slap it away from them. God's heart is broken; He is rejected by the very people He extends His love to. He walked this earth and demonstrated His transcendent love by going to the cross and giving His life. Every person has a body; God's body was named Jesus. The name Christ means "anointed one."

Therefore, the anointing power of God rested upon Jesus' body. The demonstration of God's love for us is greater than any story of a prince charming who rescued the princess. We are God's Royal Priesthood. If a human prince charming can rescue his princess, there is no doubt our Heavenly Father will come and rescue us. He has provided a way of escape, and he gives us the freedom to choose. A word of caution: Choose wisely because we can't choose our consequences.

TRANSCENDENT LOVE

TRUE LOVE FROM THE HEART

Let me see if I can find words to express my love for you, Darling. I'll do my best. My love for you runs oh, so deep. Yes, deeper than the deepest ocean or sea. It started more than 50 years ago, and over the years I've seen it grow.

I've stood by you and proved that my love is true. My love is not based upon what you can do. God put His love deep in my heart, and then I did my part. I began to read God's word and pray, and I yielded to the Holy Spirit to show me the way. You see, I knew God's love was true, and only God could direct me in loving you.

The words I write are straight from my heart. Honey, my love for you will never part. Sweetheart, you mean much more to me than I can ever express in words, you see. My love for you is bubbling inside, and I just want you to realize my love for you is not in and out or up and down, but my love for you is sound. Solid as a rock and here to stay; this is how I feel, come what may.

This is not an infatuation, for my love is true, and you don't have to guess about it, because I've proved it to you. There was a time in our marriage when we were drifting apart. The only thing that kept us together was true love in our hearts.

At one point in our marriage, the devil came and tried to take our love away. But I praise God, the Holy Spirit intervened, and the devil couldn't have his way. Yes, we've been thru the storm and rain, but by the Grace of God, honey we overcame. Yes, we've been through stormy weather, but the most important thing is we stayed together.

Our marriage is in God's hands, and I know He has the perfect plan. And as we seek Him day by day, and in our marriage allow him to have his way. Then I know we can't fail, tho the enemy sends storms straight from the pit of hell.

Like an eagle that soars high, that's the kind of love we have, you and I. When the storms of life begin to blow, we spread our love like wings and away we go!

True Love for My Darling Husband, Straight from My Heart. Composed by Carolyn Lee, February 1997 (1st Place Winner of Heart 2 Heart Romantic Poem Contest). Revised March 2024.

~PONDERING MOMENTS~

CHAPTER 11

AN INVITATION TO EXPERIENCE THE MIRACLE

When God created man, He put him to sleep, took a rib, and made woman. Woman was made whole, nothing missing, nothing broken. God said it was not good that man be alone; therefore, He made woman to complete man. No wonder the word of God says that he who finds a wife finds a good thing and obtains favor because a wife adds to the man. Men are givers; women are receivers. Anything man gives a woman, she adds to it. If a man gives her sperm, she adds children. If he provides food, she can make a meal. If he gives her a house, she can make a home. Women were created to multiply whatever man gives to her. Women makes man whole; without her, he is incomplete.

Every quality that was needed to be a husband was put inside of man at the very beginning. Also, everything that was needed to be a wife was already inside of the woman. Man should allow God to lead him to the rib He has for him. And woman should allow God to lead her to the body that has been broken for her. From the very beginning, man sacrificed for woman, who in turn accepted the sacrifice and made it productive.

Only God can take your marriage and make a miracle out of it. The word of God says little becomes much when you place it in the master's hands. The first thing you must be willing to do is place yourself completely in God's hands. The focus must be on yourself, despite what your spouse may or may not be doing. You see, you can't change your spouse, so step back and allow God to do a work in them. Ask God to search your heart. Ask Him to reveal you to you. When God reveals areas that need to be changed, be quick to repent and ask God to help you make the adjustment that's needed. Be honest with God, and be honest with yourself. Don't operate out of yourself; allow God freedom to operate through you. No marriage on earth will ever be perfect, but Praise God, it can be whole!

Operate in the forgiveness God has granted you when it comes to your spouse. Unforgiveness will block you from experiencing the miracle God has for your marriage. Remember, sin is sin in God's eyes; don't allow the enemy to plant thoughts in your mind when you are trying to rationalize what the wrong is and how it's been done instead of surrendering it completely to God. If you choose not to forgive, you will continue to experience hurt and defeat. Remember, you married your spouse because you loved them; something has happened to affect that love. You see, you are not fighting a natural battle. Everything, and I mean everything, that's done in the natural, something is happening in the spirit realm that you can't see with your natural eye. When you learn to change your focus, looking past your spouse in the natural and seeing the enemy in the spiritual realm orchestrating the confusion, your battle is half won.

Many truths have been presented in this book. You are accountable for what has been revealed to you. God wants us to understand He has a Divine order. When it's violated, we open the door to Satan to destroy our families. Remember, God placed man as the head; therefore, if the wife dominates and takes control over the man, we are out of order. When God placed Adam and Eve in the garden, he provided everything they needed. There was only one request: not to eat from the tree of knowledge of good and evil. This order was set in place to protect them when Satan entered the garden with lies of deception. Man disobeyed God and opened the door to sin and chaos. We must beware of changing the order God has set in place for our families. Women, God has blessed us with wisdom and influence. It is imperative that we seek God for direction regarding how to protect our families. This is very important because our marriage is the first example our children witness of how to interact in relationships. They hear what we think they don't and pay close attention to how we treat each other. Our interactions with each other are molding and shaping them for life. God is also taking note, and we will be held accountable.

Let me invite you to imagine for a moment: You just finished your time of prayer. You are sitting in your quiet place reading the word of God. You are interrupted by the sound of your doorbell ringing. You go to the door. You are amazed and speechless. You close your eyes and open them again, and there is an angel standing there dressed in all white with a halo. You can hardly see; the light is so dazzling bright. The angel begins to speak; his voice is like still water that penetrates deep within. He announces, "I have been assigned to deliver this personal invitation to you." As you take the invitation, the angel vanishes. You open the invitation; the letters seem to enlarge, giving you an intense feeling of urgency. It reads, "I have been watching you for some time, and your prayers have ascended as sweet aroma into my presence. My child, I see your tears and your frustrations regarding the struggles you are encountering in your marriage. You have been asking for answers and directions.

I have strategically placed a book entitled *Transcendent Love: The Restoration of a Broken Marriage* in your pathway. Please accept this invitation to allow the Holy Spirit to guide you in how to put into practice the strategies that were revealed in this book. You see, my stamp of approval is upon this book, and as you implement the Master Plan, I will make your marriage whole again. Please RSVP before it is too late. From my view, I can see time is running out." It's signed with gold, sparkling ink by God, the One who loves you more than you love yourself.

www.ingramcontent.com/pod-product-compliance
Lightning Source LLC
Chambersburg PA
CBHW071128090426
42736CB00012B/2048